Introducing Network Analysis in Social Work

of related interest:

The Case Studies for Practice series

Day Services for People with Mental Handicaps 2nd edition
Compiled by Philip Seed
ISBN 1 85302 039 7
Case Studies for Practice 1

Day Services for People with Severe Handicaps
Compiled by Philip Seed
ISBN 1 85302 013 3
Case Studies for Practice 2

Towards Independent Living:
Issues for Different Client Groups
Compiled by Philip Seed
ISBN 1 85302 018 4
Case Studies for Practice 3

HIV and AIDS:
A Social Network Approach
Compiled by Roger Gaitley and edited by Philip Seed
ISBN 1 85302 025 7
Case Studies for Practice 4

Victims of Confusion
Case Studies of Elderly Sufferers from Confusion and Dementia
Alyson Leslie
ISBN 1 85302 040 0
Case Studies for Practice 5

Social Work in the Wake of Disaster
Compiled by David Tumelty and edited by Philip Seed
ISBN 1 85302 060 5
Case Studies for Practice 6

Respite - A Social Network Approach
Philip Seed
ISBN 1 85302 061 3
Case Studies for Practice 7

Introducing Network Analysis in Social Work

Philip Seed

Jessica Kingsley Publishers
London

First published in 1990 by
Jessica Kingsley Publishers
118 Pentonville Road
London N1 9JN

British Library Cataloguing in Publication Data
Seed, Philip
Introducing network analysis in social work.
  1. Social services. Research. Methodology
  I. Title
  361'.0072

ISBN 1-85302-034-6

CONTENTS

Preface

This book has taken several months to publish since the manuscript was completed. In the intervening period, the Government's White Paper 'Care in the Community' has appeared and preparations are in progress for the implementation of the new legislation between 1991 and 1993. It is clear that an understanding of social networks, especially of home-based networks around informal care, will be central to the successful new approach to social care and case management which is envisaged.

At proof stage, I have decided to make minimal alterations to make essential links between the basic material this book presents and specific questions about case management. The book already addresses many of the issues which will face practitioners and managers implementing the new policies. For example, assessment procedures using network analysis are discussed in Chapter 5 and some of the specific questions raised by people leaving long-stay hospitals are discussed in Chapter 7. More importantly, the general approach both to understanding and enhancing client's and carer's networks will be helpful to everyone concerned with the new approach.

However, I am aware that a further book will be called for, once the new policies are in place. This will deal with assessment; case management including resource and costing issues; case finding; monitoring; and evaluation, within the overall insights that network analysis, linked with other approaches, provides. New social legislation offers, at best, a framework for change. The key practice issues will only begin to have an impact after April 1991.

The applications of social network analysis go beyond 'Care in the Community', which is defined as concerning only work with adults. This present book will be helpful especially to those working in child care, which is not covered by the new community care legislation.

Chapter 1

Introduction

Social network analysis provides a new perspective on social work and, with it, a new set of methods. These are not entirely new. They are based on an old social work intuition, namely the intuition to emphasise the 'social' in social work.

Social network analysis in social work is based on the proposition that working with a client - any client in any setting - only makes good sense if it incorporates an understanding of the client's world from the client's point of view. Specifically, this means an understanding of the people, places and activities that are important in daily living (see Figure 1). The idea of a social network offers a precise way of talking about the client's world. It is an idea, moreover, which carries with it the suggestion that other people, besides the social worker, may already be involved in helping the client. For example, a son or daughter may be an important part of the network of a client who is elderly. A sister or brother may feature prominently in the life of a disabled person. An aunt may be an important part of a child's network. In some cases, neighbours or key people in a neighbourhood feature prominently. Social workers will have become increasingly aware of these possibilities in recent years because of the emphasis now being placed on making use of informal helping networks. Social work intervention should promote and sustain already existing informal helping networks or, where they are non-existent, help them to come into being.

Social network analysis provides a way of identifying and understanding the features of social networks. More than this, it helps social workers to think in terms of how clients value other people in daily living. It is in these senses that it emphasises the 'social' in social work.

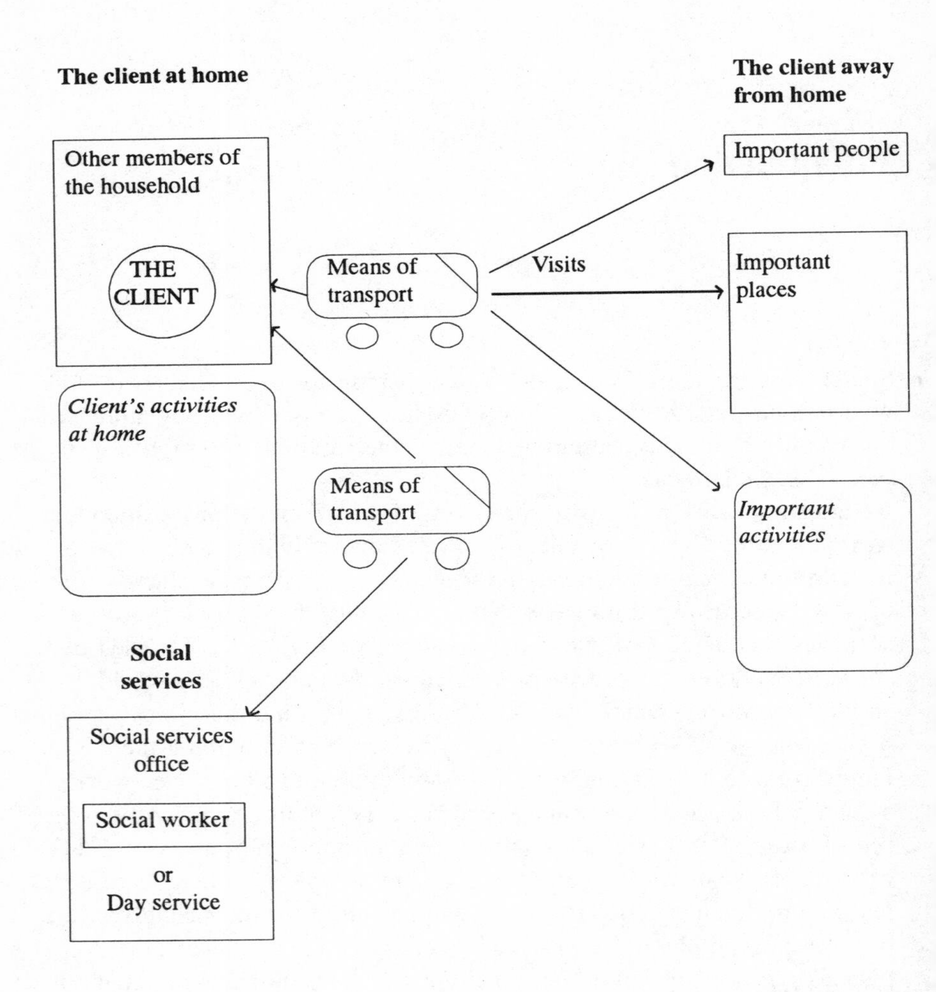

Figure 1: 'Working with a client only makes sense if it incorporates an understanding of the client's world'

Apart from people, social network analysis takes into account places and activities. People, places and activities often inter-relate. Sometimes a place is important, like a building where a club is held. A building can be important because it is the place where the client meets new people and engages in new activities. Sometimes people are important only in the context of a particular activity or, sometimes, they are important regardless of the activity - or the place. Close relations or friends, for example, may be important as people quite independent of any activity or place.

Social network analysis, then, offers precision in thinking about important aspects of social work. It has advantages over a systems approach, although the idea of the 'system' overlaps with the idea of 'network'. A system is often represented as a network. This may include the 'client system' and the 'action system'. Social network analysis gives landscape to these systems. A social network has given features: people, places and activities. There will be different kinds of people, different kinds of places and different kinds of activities, all of which constitute the social landscape of people's lives. Social work intervention should concern itself with an understanding of this landscape.

Let me give an example.

> An elderly person is referred to a newly established day centre because, it is felt, she is lonely. But what evidence is there that she is lonely? Did she tell the social worker this? Did the social worker infer it from other information? If we have a way of systematically studying the elderly person's pattern of living, or social landscape, we shall have firmer evidence and not just hearsay.

The evidence is based partly on a diary.

One of the discoveries that my colleagues and I have made from research and practice based on social network analysis is that social work clients, on the whole, enjoy keeping diaries. They do not often regard it as an imposition and they do not even, very often, find it particularly difficult. Of course some clients will need help in keeping diaries and this in itself is interesting because it brings into prominence the person, whoever it is, who constitutes what we call 'the main support person'. Everyone has someone in their lives who can be called the main support person.

In the case of the elderly lady who had been referred to a day centre, the main support person was her friend who lived in another flat in the same building. During a monitored period, as we call it - in this case four weeks - when daily diaries were kept, the elderly lady saw her friend 32 times. Well, to cut this story short, she was far from isolated - though she may still have told the truth to a social worker who asked 'do you sometimes feel lonely?' But further investigation using social network analysis revealed that if she went to a day centre, without her friend doing the same, she would actually tend to lose the contact she already had. When her interests and pattern of living had been thoroughly investigated, it also transpired that the only tangible benefit to her in going to a day centre would have been access to a tumble drier - which neither she nor her friend possessed.

The information from diaries is presented in the form of a network diagram. Figure 2 shows a diagram drawn from the diaries in the case we have just considered. Part of the value of producing a diagram is that it enables us to compare two or more patterns of living of clients whose circumstances - or structure for living as we may call it - are similar. Many such contrasts have been given in the *Case Studies for Practice* series which can usefully be considered alongside this present volume.

In the first part of this book the social worker is given a description and explanation of the methods of social network analysis. Firstly (Chapter 2) we review what is currently known about social networks. We describe in more detail what we have called the social landscape of people's lives. We are particularly concerned to ask about the sources of help and satisfaction for clients. Satisfaction is often derived from helping others and one of the benefits of social network analysis is that it enables us to focus on this aspect and not merely on client needs in terms of dependency on others. Mutual support amongst friends as well as neighbours is, in some instances, still very real, despite an assumption amongst some writers that it is a thing of the past. On the other hand, many people today do live isolated and lonely lives and these may benefit from the efforts to arrange contacts, support and friendships which feature increasingly in social work today.

We then consider (Chapter 3) how social networks, with this varied landscape, can be most usefully analysed for social work practice. There are many ways of looking at networks which we shall draw upon. One of the pioneers in this field was herself (amongst other things) a social worker, namely Elizabeth Bott. Through studying social networks, she discovered in the 1950s that features of marital roles and relationships had a bearing on the husband's or wife's activities outside the home. Unfortunately for

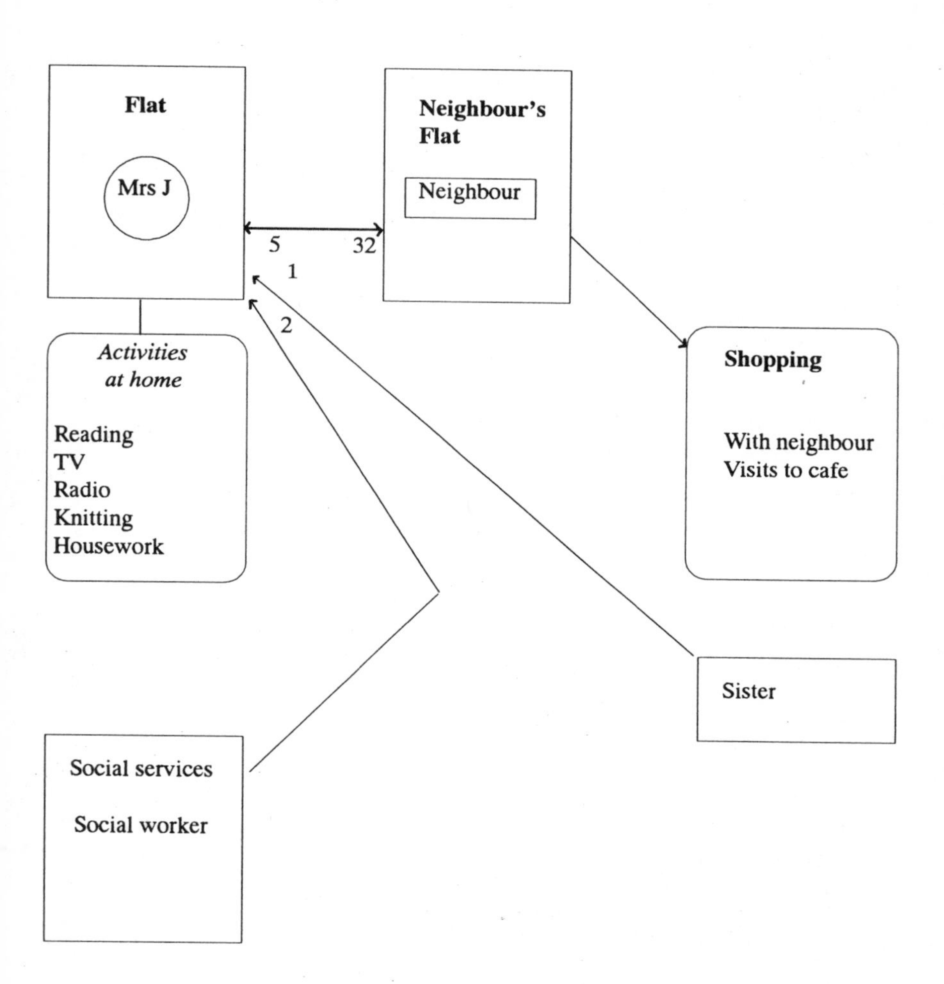

Figure 2: Network diagram based on a diary kept by an elderly client, Mrs J, for 28 days

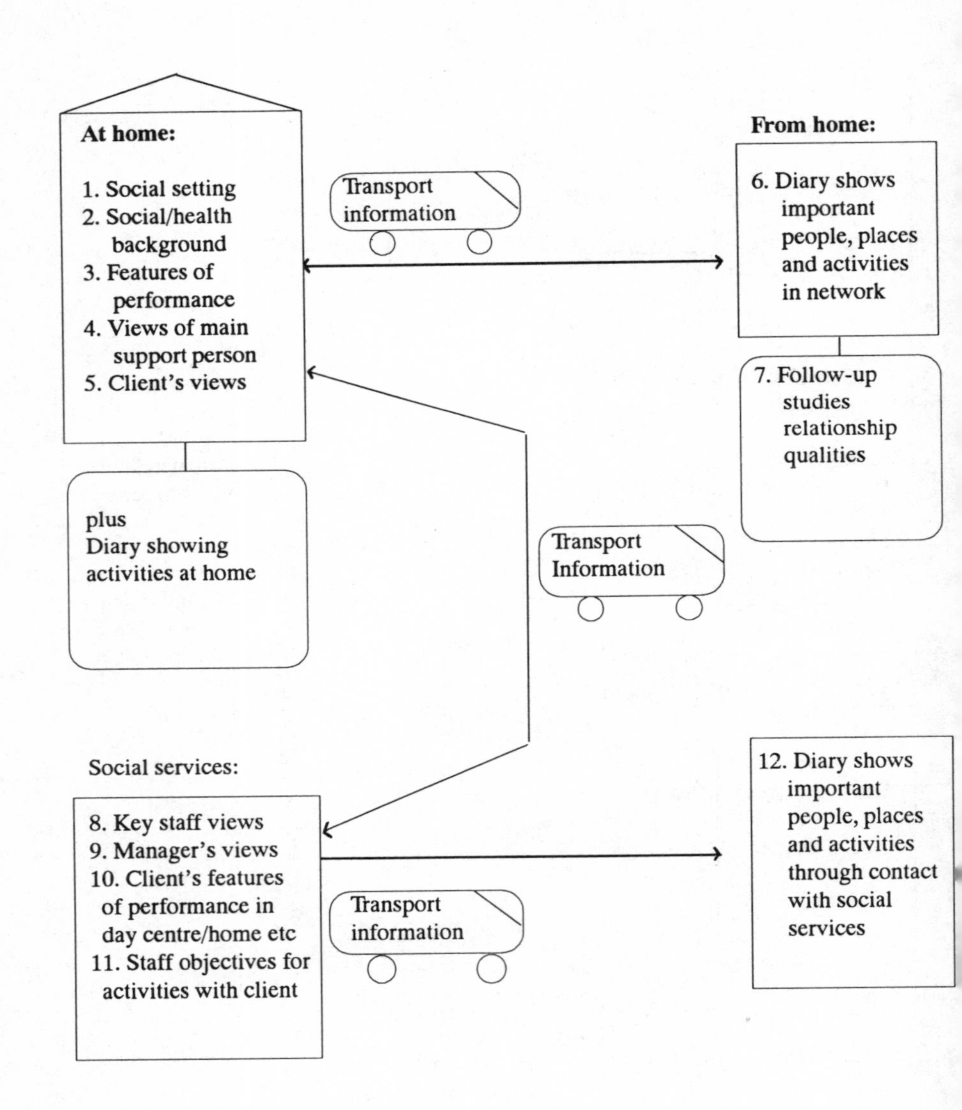

Figure 3: The main information components of network analysis

social work, Elizabeth Bott's findings and her approach became more seriously taken up by academic sociologists than by practising social workers. The result has been an increasingly theoretical literature on methods of analysing network structures whose applications to social work have been at best peripheral. It is necessary to draw out from this literature specific ideas about measurable components of what we call 'relationship qualities'. Sociological notions of roles such as 'instrumental' and 'affective', help us to define specific qualities in relationships which take us beyond such traditional social work descriptions of relationships as 'supportive', or 'good'.

Finally in Part 1 (Chapter 4) we describe the various techniques and skills that the social worker must learn in order to practice network analysis. We have already referred to the diaries, but these are only part of the total process of gathering information. For example, other information components that are needed include details of the client's social setting and social background, features of his or her performance in daily living, details of what the client thinks about the services and of what social work staff themselves feel about the service they are providing. Figure 3 outlines the main components we are concerned with.

All this information is gathered by means of interview schedules. A schedule is different from a questionnaire. A questionnaire requires limited responses, contained within the question. The responses we try to get from schedules are disciplined in the sense that there is structure to them but they are not restricted. They are open ended. Experience in using these schedules has emphasised their value in helping the social worker to look at his/her work through the client's perspective as well as through the perspective of the agency.

Part 2 of this book considers specific applications. Social network analysis has both prospective and retrospective uses. Its prospective uses include preparing for future placements and playing a part in referral and assessment procedures. From the point of view of social work management, social network analysis also has a predictive use in projecting future needs, not just for individual clients but for groups of clients or for services as a whole in a given neighbourhood. Its retrospective uses include reviews and the evaluation of outcomes based on previous plans. These prospective and retrospective uses apply in various situations. In Chapter 5 we consider their use in field work assessments, e.g. in a range of situations where field workers make an initial assessment following a referral. In Chapter 6 we look at assessments in residential settings, especially prior to discharge. In Chapter 7 we consider the particular issues which a social network analysis highlights in working with people who leave long-stay hospitals. Chapter 8 looks specifically at day services and Chapter 9 takes a broad look at other applications in service development, illustrated by procedure for a client-needs led approach to setting up a new day service.

The use of social network analysis in social work is at a relatively early stage. A number of seminars have been held under the auspices of the Central Council for Education and Training in Social Work (in Scotland) and the methods taught are gradually being introduced in a range of different agencies and settings. One of the immediate benefits to their work reported by seminar participants is that the methods forced them to be aware of features of the clients' lives and views in ways which were previously hidden from them. Moreover, in some cases, the exercise, and especially the keeping of diaries, enabled clients to improve their ability to communicate, not only with social workers but with others. Some problems were also reported. One was that it is difficult to incorporate the methods we are proposing unless 'everyone else does it' in a given office or area. In other words, it is recognised that the use of these particular methods involves procedures which do not just concern the isolated social worker but others in the social work collaborative process. We do not apologise for this because it is one of the intentions of network analysis that the collaborative aspects of social work should be emphasised. At the same time we recognise that there are problems of implementation for groups of social workers and for agencies. We hope that further seminars will be held on an agency and inter-agency basis in association with the use of the material supplied in this book and from the *Case Studies for Practice* series. The author and his team, as well as the publisher, will be happy to collaborate and offer suggestions for the organisation of seminars and in providing teaching material.

Part One

General

Chapter 2

What are social networks?

'Network' is a term which is widely used today in very different contexts. This was brought home to me when I was talking to my son, who is an electrical engineer, about the fact that I was writing a book on network analysis. He promptly took from his shelf a book of his own entitled *Network Analysis*. It was all about electrical circuits! As I sit in my study writing this book, I have in front of me another volume entitled *Applied Network Analysis*. This one is full of mathematical and statistical formulae which are intelligible chiefly, if not solely, to a particular school of sociologists. Again, if I turn to my computer manual I find references to networks of an entirely different kind.

What, then, is a network? And what, in particular, is a social network?

A network is a system or pattern of links between points, usually shown in a diagram, which have particular meanings. In my son's electrical engineering book, the points were things like transformers and rectifiers and the links represented electric currents. In social networks, the points are people, places where people meet or activities that people pursue. The links, or 'lines' as we call them, represent the journeys that people undertake to meet other people, to visit places or engage in activities.

People, places and activities interrelate but sometimes each can have a distinct significance. For example, some people are important because they are associated with a particular place or a particular activity. Sometimes an activity is important because it is associated with a particular place. On the other hand, activities may be important - perhaps jogging for example or cycling - without particular reference to the place where the activity is

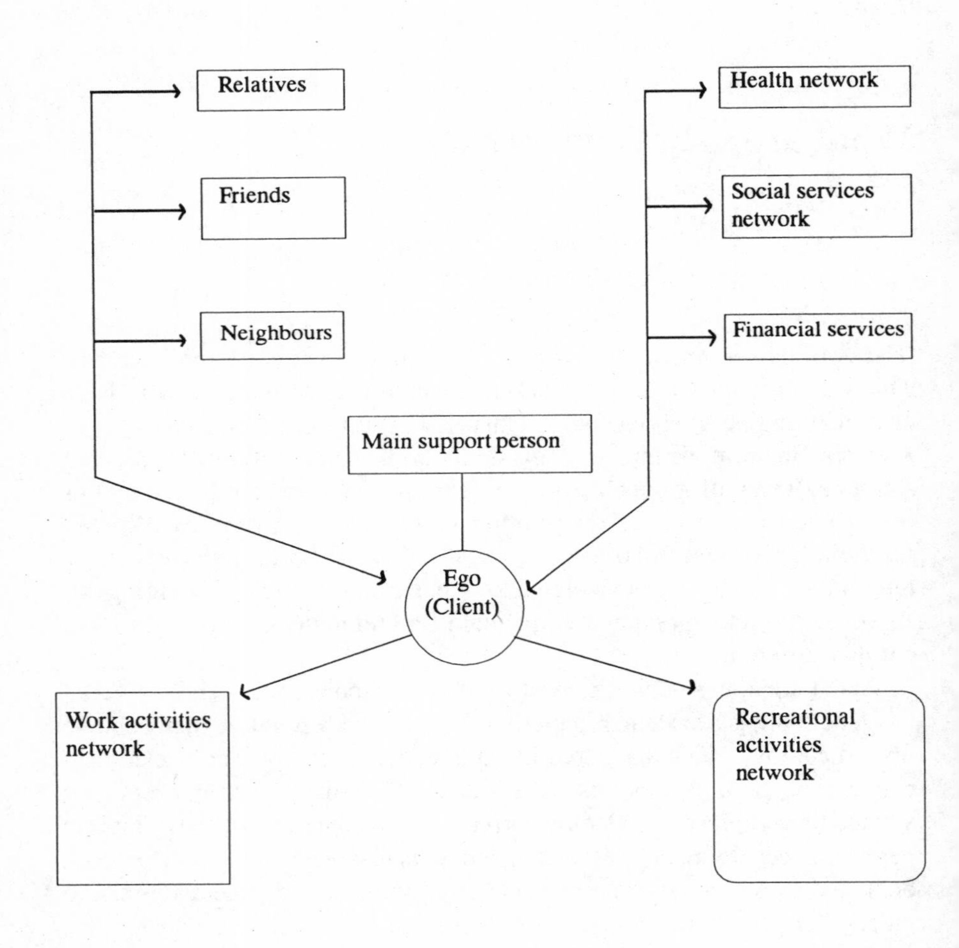

Figure 4: The Ego-centred network

undertaken. Close friends may be important irrespective of any particular activity or place.

The networks which social workers are concerned with will focus on one (or more) client(s) in relation to one (or more) social service agency(ies) *in the context of the client's pattern of daily living*. Within this 'pattern' specific kinds of networks can be identified. These include 'home-based' networks, 'work-based' networks, 'health-based' networks and 'recreation networks'. These possibilities are illustrated in Figure 4.

The network depicted in Figure 4 focuses on one particular client. It is an example of what sociologists call an 'Ego-centred' network. It centres round 'Ego' who, in this case, is the client. 'Ego' has friends. These friends may or may not be in touch with one another. An Ego-centred network is not particularly concerned with the relationships which do not directly involve 'Ego'.

Social workers might be concerned with networks concerning a group rather than a single Ego. For example, in social work we might particularly be concerned with a network comprising some, or all, of the residents of a children's home, a home for elderly people or perhaps a residential school.

Figure 5 outlines the possibilities for another kind of network. It is assumed the social worker is working with an intermediate treatment (IT) group. He or she might be particularly interested to know how far the members of the group are in contact with one another outside the formal group sessions and what sorts of activities they engage in.

Figure 6 takes this exercise a stage further. Let us suppose that the sessions of the IT group are suspended. To what extent are the activities of members of the group sustained in the absence of formal group sessions? In other words, to what extent do the members attending the group constitute a social network?

It should be noticed from Figure 5 that one of the members, Bert, was not in fact attending the IT sessions, although he was formally a member. In Figure 6, however, when the group is suspended, he suddenly becomes a key person in the network of the group attenders. Bill, Mary, Joe and Henry all visit him at home, sometimes directly from home and sometimes after they have been to the cafe.

These considerations raise the further question of the difference between a group and a network. The two concepts overlap but perhaps the differences can be summarised as follows:

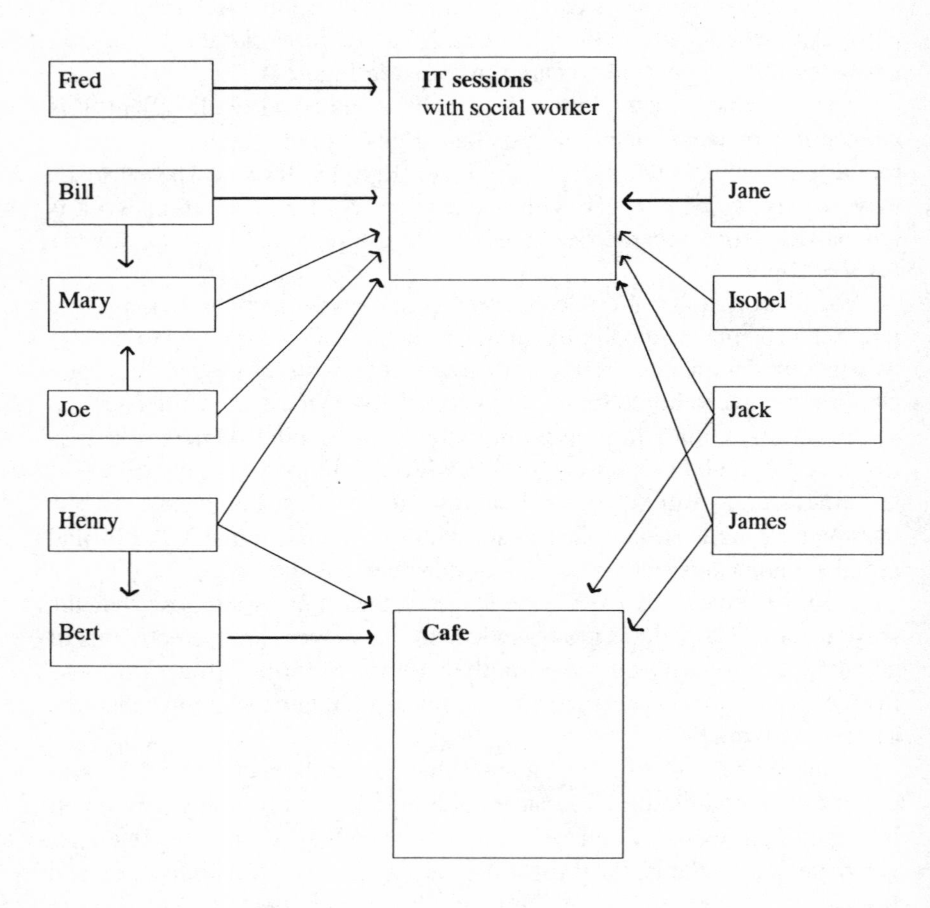

Figure 5: Network drawing showing contacts between members of an IT group

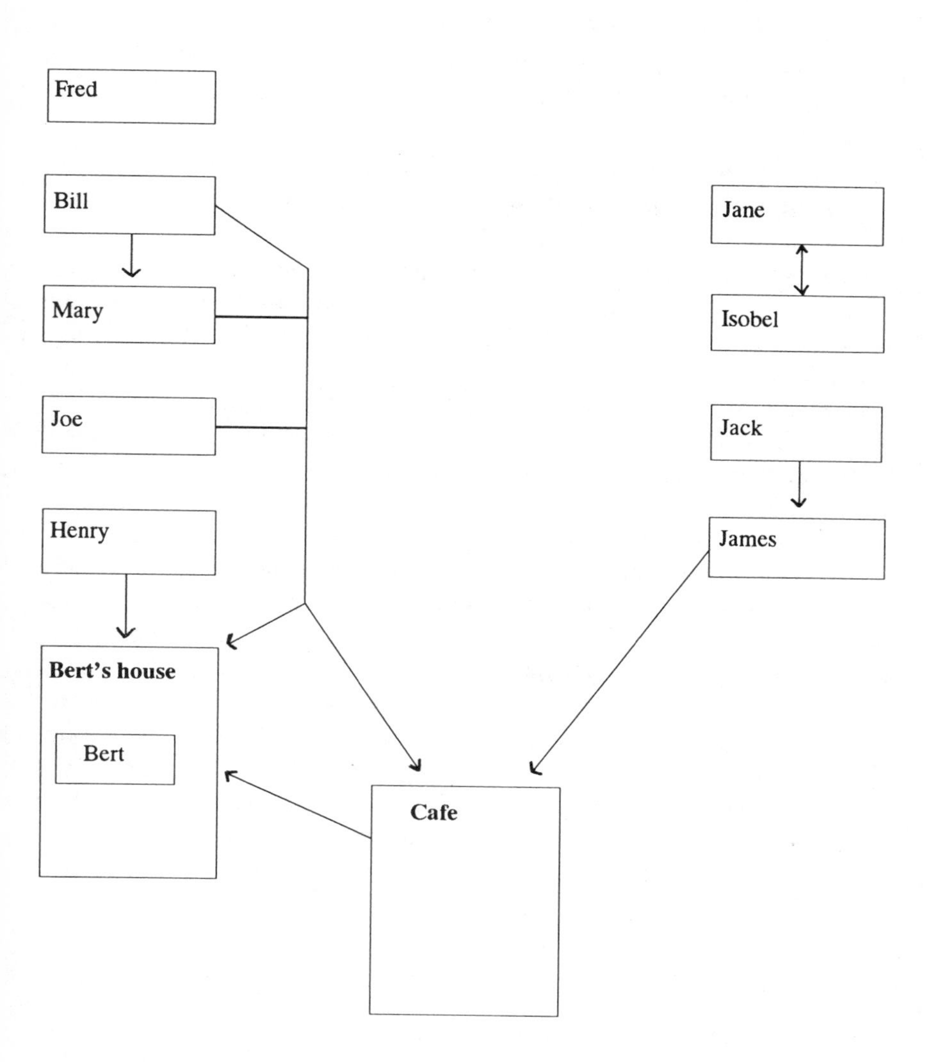

Figure 6: Network drawing showing contacts between the same IT group members (see Figure 5) when group meetings are suspended for a while

A group comprises people who come together and subsequently meet together, usually on some regular basis.

A social network, more broadly, represents meaningful contact between people who do not necessarily all meet together or even all know one another.

Both groups and networks have identifiable structures and role differentiation. For example, in a group situation, there will be leaders. Leaders may be referred to as 'key people' in a network.

We can translate these differences and similarities into our own everyday experiences. A regular staff meeting is likely to be considered a group, but if we were to consider all the individuals within the total work setting and the different kinds of contacts we had with these different people, this would constitute a work based network. If we were just to consider *our* relationships with others in the work setting it would constitute an ego-centred work-based network, whereas if we were also interested in the relationships between, for example, the boss and other colleagues besides ourselves, the network would become broader.

A social network must obviously have boundaries or it would ultimately include the whole family of.man! Boundaries will be imposed depending on the purpose for which the exercise of defining networks is undertaken. For example, a health- or hospital-based social worker might be interested in looking at contacts within the hospital as these affected the client's health and well-being. A community worker might be interested in finding out about key contacts in a particular neighbourhood. Networks provide a useful context for many different social work functions. Two social work functions are particularly important, especially in community care. These are:

Assessing and supporting informal helping networks

Developing network potential

Informal helping networks

Peter Wilmott has brought together studies of social networks with a view to assessing the opportunities for informal help which such networks provide. Sources of informal help include relatives, friends, neighbours and key people in the community. Amongst other questions, he considers whether neighbourhood communities, from which informal help may be drawn, are still to be found. His general conclusion is as follows:[1]

> 'Contrary to popular belief, in present-day Britain most localities, for most people, have something of the character of a community of attachment ... local community undoubtedly matters in the lives of the great majority of people in Britain. But, also for the great majority, ties with relatives, friends and others now extend far beyond the local area, and the neighbourhood or local community does not encompass the social networks of those people ... most residents look beyond their neighbourhood for most of their social relationships, even including those most important to them.'

It is important, therefore, that social workers understand the neighbourhood communities in which their clients live. Different kinds of communities have very different kinds of features. Consider, for example, the obvious differences between, say, a tourist area and an area with an industrial manufacturing base. Or consider the differences between an inner city area and an outer suburb. These broad categories are not necessarily representative of the most important kinds of distinctions between communities. I have lived much of my life in rural communities - and I am constantly impressed by the differences between different kinds of villages. Villages, especially in modern times, have become highly specialised. I live at the moment between two villages in Scotland. One is a farming centre with a lively weekly market, or 'mart' as it is called. There are four or five places in the village where you could buy a tractor, but no chemist. There are three banks but nowhere where you could buy clothes. The other village has a long tradition of being associated with services. There are two wholesale bakeries, a chemist, two chip shops, a doctor's surgery, a vet, a bus company, a large builder and various trades people. Both villages have only a few hundred population but serve a large surrounding countryside.

The industrial base of a town or village will affect the quality of ordinary people's lives. It will also affect the extent to which people look to others outside for support, or whether they are largely self supporting.

Some communities develop and change while others remain remarkably static for a long period of years. Sudden changes brought about by external factors, such as the discovery of oil, can have profound effects on a local community. Other communities suffer when there is a steady exodus of people from them. The relevance for the social worker is often in conside-ring the characteristics of those who are most likely to be left behind. Sometimes those most able to give help to others informally are those most likely to leave while those most in need of help - the elderly and the handicapped - may be those most inclined to stay.

Our understanding of local communities needs to encompass the following kinds of questions:

What sustains the community, economically and socially?

Has it a mixed or highly specialised kind of economy?

In what ways is it vulnerable to change brought about either by the influx of new people or by the exodus of existing inhabitants?

What are the likely consequences of recent and past changes that have occurred to its social structure?

In some cases there is a cycle of events which can lead to increasing vulnerability in a community. Let us suppose a housing estate was built perhaps 20 years ago. Let us then suppose that, at a certain stage, the community becomes defined as being socially a less desirable place to live than other neighbourhoods. Professionals, and others able to do so, move out from the neighbourhood and their places are taken by others who are perhaps forced to live in that neighbourhood because they do not have the means to live elsewhere. Enterprising members of the community also leave and those that remain constitute a disproportionate number of people who are dependent on others. At the same time professionals and others most able to be the providers of informal help continue to move out.

There will be variations of this kind of scenario involving the influx of minority groups.

In view of the many forces which could be said to contribute to the decline of traditional communities with a high degree of mutual support, the surprising thing is, perhaps, people's resilience and their capacity to form compensatory networks. For example, incomers to a new estate who have severed links with the communities they have left may readily form new links based on their mutual isolation. With young families, children will often be the first to forge new links across boundary fences. In the older inner cities, bereft of their original character, children will also form links - for better or worse.

So it is that Peter Wilmott is able to write on the basis of research, 'most localities, for most people, have something of the character of a community of attachment'. However, social workers are not concerned with 'most people'. They are more likely concerned with the ones who are not 'most people'. A knowledge of what is typical for most people provides the background of an understanding of the distinctive networks of social work clients. Let me give an example, again, of children. Children in 'most cases', as we have said, cross the wall or the fence (sometimes where adults fear to tread) to meet their classmates out of school.[2] This does *not* apply, however, to children with complex learning difficulties attending special schools. Their social networks are more likely to comprise contacts with relatives than with peers at school.[1] In other words, families with handicapped members tend to depend on close relatives in offering support to the handicapped member whose life, in turn, is oriented to that support rather than to the mutual interchange that comes, in the case of normal children, from daily contacts with the kids next door. The study of networks can reveal the specific circumstances in this kind of situation and critically examine the relationship qualities of the main support people. Are they, for example, providing a relationship at the expense of opportunities for the client to engage in other activities with other people?

Developing network potential

The second possible use of networks which is commonly put forward in social work is in connection with the development of a client's network potential - in other words, his or her potential and need to develop new friends. For example, people with mental handicaps or mental illness, leaving hospital and endeavouring to develop a new life in the community, will be likely to have two kinds of needs. Firstly they are likely to have material needs; secondly they are likely to have social needs. The same would apply to anyone leaving any kind of long-stay institution, for example prison. How do they manage financially and materially? How do they make new friends? These two questions are related to one another. Without adequate financial means, many people become withdrawn and find it difficult to make new friends. They may also lack the means to travel to meet people. So how do people in these circumstances make new friends? To answer these questions it is firstly necessary to understand the kinds of social networks they had when they were institutionalised. They are likely to have had two very different kinds of very limited relationships. Firstly, they will have had limited relations with a peer group - those in the same hospital ward or in the same prison block or whatever. The relationships with their peer group will have been unusual, to say the least. Fellow patients or fellow prisoners are not the same as next door neighbours. One is forced into confinement with fellow patients or fellow prisoners. Patients and prisoners lack the opportunity to go out and make friends with others whose presence is not forced upon them. The same applies to the second category of relationships which patients and prisoners share, namely, the relationships with those in authority over them, including helping professionals.

I once studied the network of a lady who had graduated successfully from hospital to a half-way house and then on to 'independent living' in a flat. This was over a period of many years. It was interesting to discover that after this long time nearly all her relationships in the community were still either with ex-patients or with professionals.

We therefore have to understand our client's previous experiences of social networks and then consider their present patterns of living before asking the question; how can they be helped to extend the networks they have? Developing network potential - or networking, as it is sometimes called - puts together our knowledge of the client's individual network experience, past and present, with knowledge of the network potential of the local community in which the client lives. How can the client, with his limitations and potential, tap into the resources, limited or extensive as they may be, which are to be found in the neighbourhood outside? Having studied these questions we can then consider what active networking might entail.

'Networking' has sometimes had a technical meaning (in the United States particularly) of bringing together important people within the client's network to help to solve problems facing either the client himself or herself, or the dependent relative. For example, this might be appropriate in the case of deciding the best course of action in a crisis situation where an elderly carer of a handicapped son or daughter has himself or herself suffered perhaps an accident and is no longer able to cope. Various relatives have an interest in the situation. Should one or another of them take over the burden of caring or should some form of institutional care be considered? Networking in this context might mean bringing together the relevant people with a social worker (or social workers) and conducting a meeting or a series of meetings to resolve the crisis.

However, I propose to use the concept of networking more broadly to include any action to develop, sustain or utilise the client's network potential. This might include the kind of meeting between key people described above. Alternatively, it might involve accompanying the client, for example an elderly person recently bereaved, in making new friends and taking advantage of new social opportunities by joining clubs or developing interests. Various voluntary groups have now built up substantial experience in befriending different client groups including children in care, children and adults with special needs, people with mental health problems, the elderly and so on. The support of informal help in the community and development of the client's network potential illustrates the obvious uses of an understanding of social networks. The central proposition in this book is that an understanding of social networks is helpful in everyday social work with clients in everyday situations.

References

1. Wilmott, P., (1986), *Social Networks Informal Care and Public Policy*, Policy Studies Institute.

2. Evidence of this was found in a study by the author (unpublished) into social aspects of integration sponsored by the Scottish Education Department. A shortened version is forthcoming in Jones, N., (Ed) *Special Needs Review*, vol. II, Falmer Press, 1990.

Discussion exercises

1. Write down the main features of the communities where (a) you live and (b) you work. If they are not one and the same, which do you know most about?

2. Suppose a house for adults with learning difficulties was being opened in your home locality and you were approached as a key person by the staff to help the residents to find new friends. How could you respond?

Chapter 3

What is analysis?

A social network is a representation. It is not a 'real thing' like an elephant or a blade of grass. It is a way of representing people's patterns of daily living and, in particular, the people, places and activities that are significant. A representation in the form of a network is used to facilitate interpretation and analysis.

A network is like a map. A map is produced in order that it can be interpreted with the aid of a key. A social network is a social map. Instead of roads, railways and bridges or forests it represents the social landscape of people's lives.

Network analysis in social work, however, is broader than interpreting the data represented on a network drawing. The network drawing is in some ways the centre-piece but we also need to know information about the client's social setting and social background, about his or her features of performance in daily living and about the views of the client, as well as the views of key people who feature in his or her daily life.

Some of the terms we have just used require further explanation.

Social setting

When we collect information or data about the client's social setting we are concerned with the following:

- A description of the accommodation where the client lives and of the immediate neighbourhood environment.
- Information about who shares the accommodation with the client.

- The identity of close relatives or friends, currently in contact with the client, but who do not live with the client.
- Details of means of transport available to the client.
- Access to key community facilities, e.g. the post office, essential shopping, General Practitioner, sport and leisure facilities.
- Details of domiciliary support available to the client through formal or informal services.

Social history

This will include the following:

- A history of the client's previous accommodation.
- A history of schooling.
- An occupational history of the client since leaving school.
- A history of relevant health problems and disabilities.
- A history of any relevant social or behavioural problems.

Features of performance

The features of performance which we are concerned with mainly concern:

(a) Self management skills

(b) Daily living skills.

(c) Social skills.

We are also interested in performance related to the client's particular interests.

By 'self management' skills we mean things like getting dressed and undressed, washing, bathing, using the toilet, eating and drinking, getting about and basic communication with others. These are sometimes called basic tasks.

By 'daily living' skills we mean accomplishing the more complex tasks that daily living entails, such as the following:

- preparing food and drink for self and for others

- performing household tasks
- understanding, using and managing money
- using public transport

We are also concerned with social skills, such as the ability to respond to the needs and wishes of others and to understand others' feelings.

Many of the items listed above feature on check lists for performance assessments with which many social workers will be familiar. For purposes of network analysis, however, we have developed our own particular approach to collecting this kind of information. This is not in the form of a check list; it is more like a description of the *features* of how the client performs, or finds difficulty in performing, in self management, daily living and social tasks. It is concerned with explanations of difficulties in a social context. This point will be discussed in more detail in the next chapter.

Views

Client views are incorporated in network analysis in two ways. Firstly, the client will be asked to keep diaries; these diaries may include not just factual recordings of events but comments on these events. Secondly, we will be asking the client for his or her views on the following:

Accommodation, including the people he or she lives with, the space available, the convenience of the location and so on.

Place of work or other occupation or day-time activity. This will include the question 'Would you like to do something else?' If the answer is 'yes', then, 'What would you prefer to do instead?'

Other activities and interests including the question 'Are there other things you would like to do but do not get the chance to do?'

In situations where the client is dependent (as most of us are) on someone whom we call a 'main support person', we also ask that person for their understanding of the client's views and some additional questions relating to the support that they themselves receive. Similar questions will also be asked of the social worker or others providing an important service to the client.

Each of these main groups of topics are called 'Information Components'. They are the components needed to provide a detailed knowledge of the context for understanding the client's social network. (See Figure 3.)

Let us now come to the analysis of the network itself. There are three dimensions to the analysis of social networks in social work. These are:

- Network features
- Network types
- Relational content (relationship qualities)

Network features

Let us consider a network for a fortnight in the life of a client called Jack (Figure 7). Jack has just left school and is on social work supervision. The features of Jack's network include the following:

Home base

Jack lives with his mother, step-father and baby half-sister.

Occupation base

Jack is on a Youth Training Scheme. He works six days during the fortnight in a store and attends college twice (the other days he does not attend).

Contacts with relations

Jack has contact with his granny. She visits the house twice and Jack visits granny's house six times during the fortnight.

Friends

Jack has no friends at work or at college but he does have a group of friends whom he meets almost daily at a cafe.

Activities

Jack has very few activities in his life. He spends a lot of time listening to records, both at home and at the cafe. On one occasion Jack and his friends

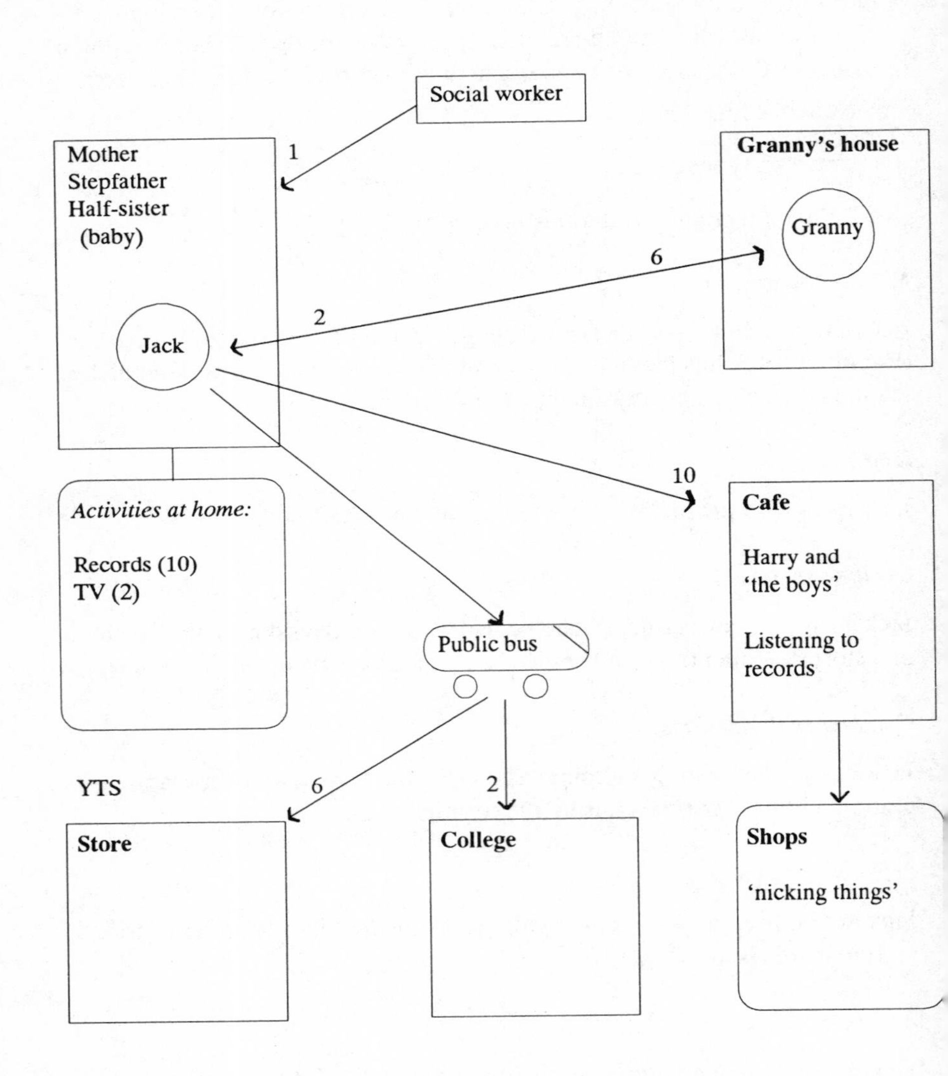

Figure 7: A fortnight in Jack's life

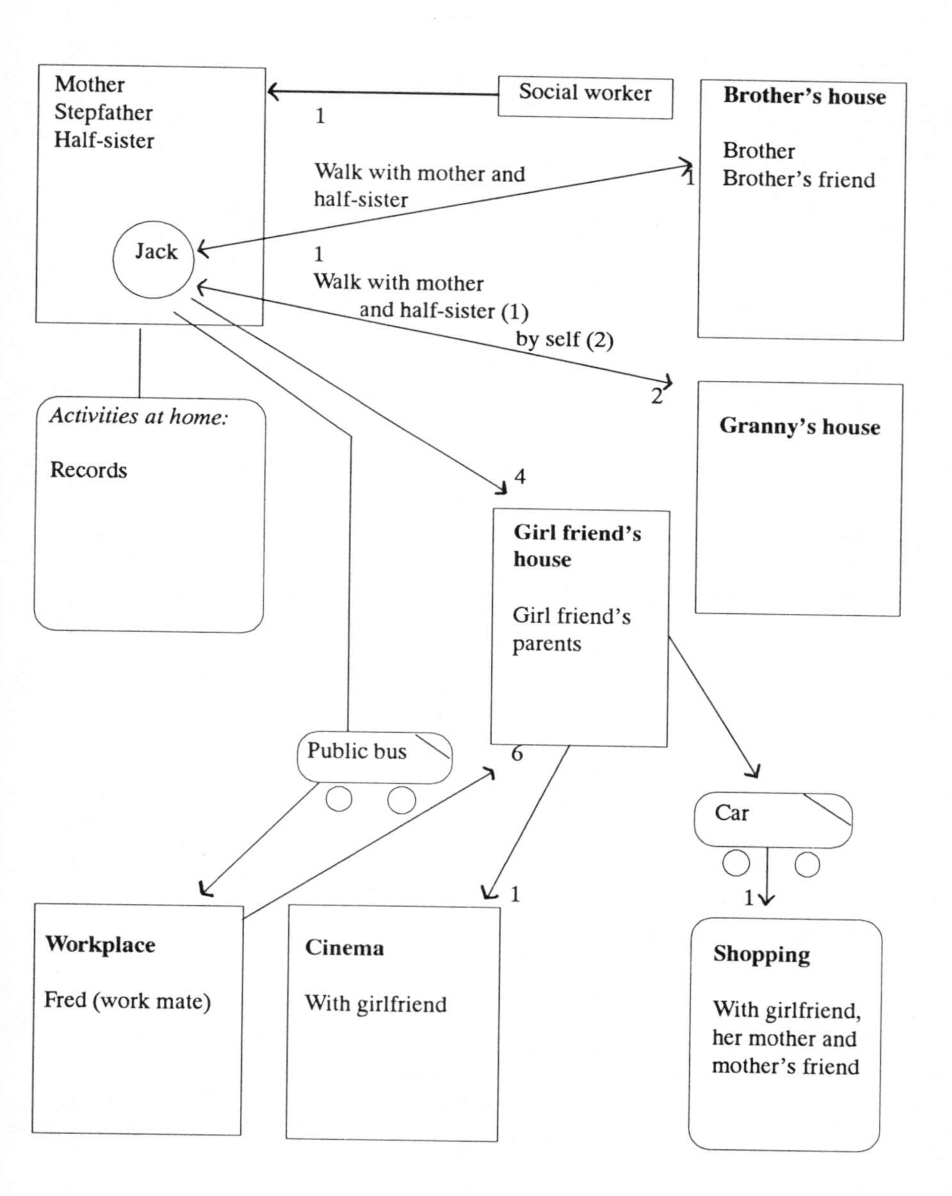

Figure 8: A fortnight in Jack's life, one year later

go out on a visit to the shops. Jack is able to record in his diary that they were nicking things. (They were not caught!)

Social work input

The social worker visits once during the fortnight.

The statements in brackets in the above list can be obtained from background information components, but the other information comes directly from the diaries in the network drawing. Classifying data from the networks has value, firstly, in so far as it enables us to compare Jack's pattern of living from what one would expect, i.e. what might be considered more normal and socially acceptable. Secondly, it enables us to see what are the strengths and deficits in Jack's network compared with what one might expect. Thirdly, we can compare his network with other clients in similar situations, i.e. other youngsters on supervision. Finally, we can make comparisons between Jack's network at the present time, and, say, in a year's time. Jack's network a year later is shown in Figure 8. Let us note the changes that have taken place using the headings which we used before to classify network features:

Home base

Unchanged (except, of course, everyone is a year older including Jack himself and his baby half-sister).

Occupation base

Jack has finished his YT scheme and is fortunate in having been placed in permanent employment.

Contacts with relatives

Contacts with Granny are diminished. (Granny has had an accident and is unable to visit the family home.) Instead Jack visits her, on one occasion with his mother and half-sister and on another occasion by himself. Jack also now has contact with his married brother, who did not feature in the first network shown in Figure 7. He visits his brother and their family in company with his mother and half-sister.

Contacts with friends

Jack now has a regular girlfriend and his contacts with her have displaced his previous contacts with Harry and the boys in the cafe. He also now has a friend at work called Fred.

Activities

Most of Jack's leisure activities are with his girlfriend. He still listens to records at home. He also listens to records at his girlfriend's house. Notice that his girlfriend does not visit Jack at his own home.

Social work input

The social worker still visits though less frequently.

Another feature of networks that can sometimes be important is transport. It may be noted that Jack, in the first network (Figure 7) either travels by bus or walks. In the second network he sometimes travels in his girlfriend's car. (His girlfriend, who is a year or two older than Jack, is learning to drive and Jack is accompanied by his girlfriend and his girlfriend's mother on a shopping expedition by car.)

Sometimes, though not in Jack's case, we might want to focus on a particular aspect or part of the total network. For example, we might wish to separate out a health-based network including visits to doctors, hospitals and so on; a legal-based network comprising dealings with the court, solicitors etc.; or a holiday-based network.

Network types

We have seen that network features refer to the specifics of an individual network, e.g. with what sorts of people, in what sorts of places and in what sorts of activities the client is involved.

Network *types* apply to more general features, i.e. what can we say about the network as a whole? As an exercise, try answering this question with regard to Jack's two networks. In your own words write down what strikes you about Jack's way of life as illustrated in the network drawings. Comment also on the general changes that have taken place between the first network and the second. We shall return to this at the end of the Chapter but, in the meantime, we can refer to the more general types of networks that are the results of other people's reflections on a great many other networks.

Firstly, there is the concept of *density*. This is a technical term used by social anthropologists. It refers to the question, how far are the different people who feature in the network in contact with one another? If we were interested in this question, we would need either to ask the key people who feature in the diary, i.e. in Jack's case, the granny, the girlfriend and Fred or ask them to keep diaries themselves. For example, does Granny have any contact with Jack's girlfriend or with Fred? We might assume that Granny might have some contact with Jack's married brother but it is dangerous in network analysis to make any assumptions! If we wanted to find this out, we would have to ask.

Figure 9 imagines results of a fuller kind of what may in this case be called a 'total' network analysis. The contacts between the people who feature in the network are shown by broken lines.

Jack's network is more dense than one might have expected. Fred (Jack's work-mate) is in touch with Jack's brother and Jack's brother (as we might have expected) is also in touch with their Granny. Fred, however, is also in touch with Jack's girlfriend, Mary, and perhaps, most surprisingly, there is a connection between Mary and Jack's Granny through their mutual contact with Mary's own Granny. Jack, however, has no contact with Mary's Granny. We can thus see that looking at the density adds a new dimension to the possibilities for understanding networking potential.

Some networks are characterised by a close circle of friendships which exclude others outside. This has been studied, in relation to social work, in terms of whether a network could be described as 'self-contained'. A self-contained network may or may not be a dense one and it may or may not be extensive. If a network is small and self-contained the social worker may well have cause for concern, for we all need social contacts in life. Often people whose networks are self-contained tend to be suspicious of offers of help from outside and the social worker will be aware of this. The opposite of the self-contained network is called *embracing*. Here the client typically reaches out to embrace relationships with others including people with whom they may not previously have been familiar. Often a client in this position will seek out services rather than wait for them to come to them. Jack's second network is perhaps showing some signs of becoming more embracing, or of reaching out, particularly since he has a girlfriend.

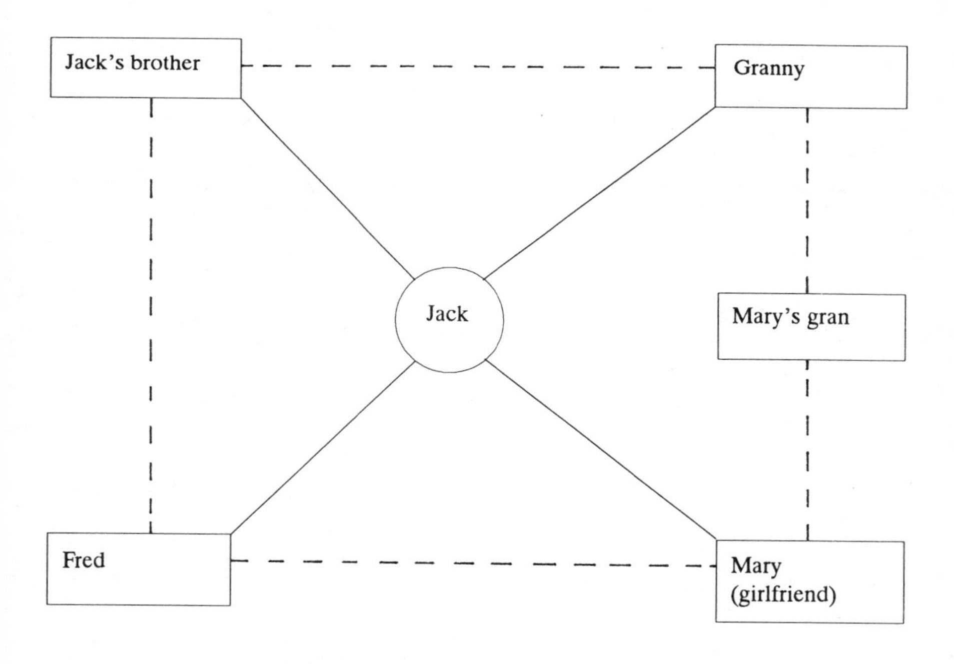

Figure 9: Diagram illustrating the density of Jack's friendship and relative's network (contacts NOT involving Jack are shown with broken lines)

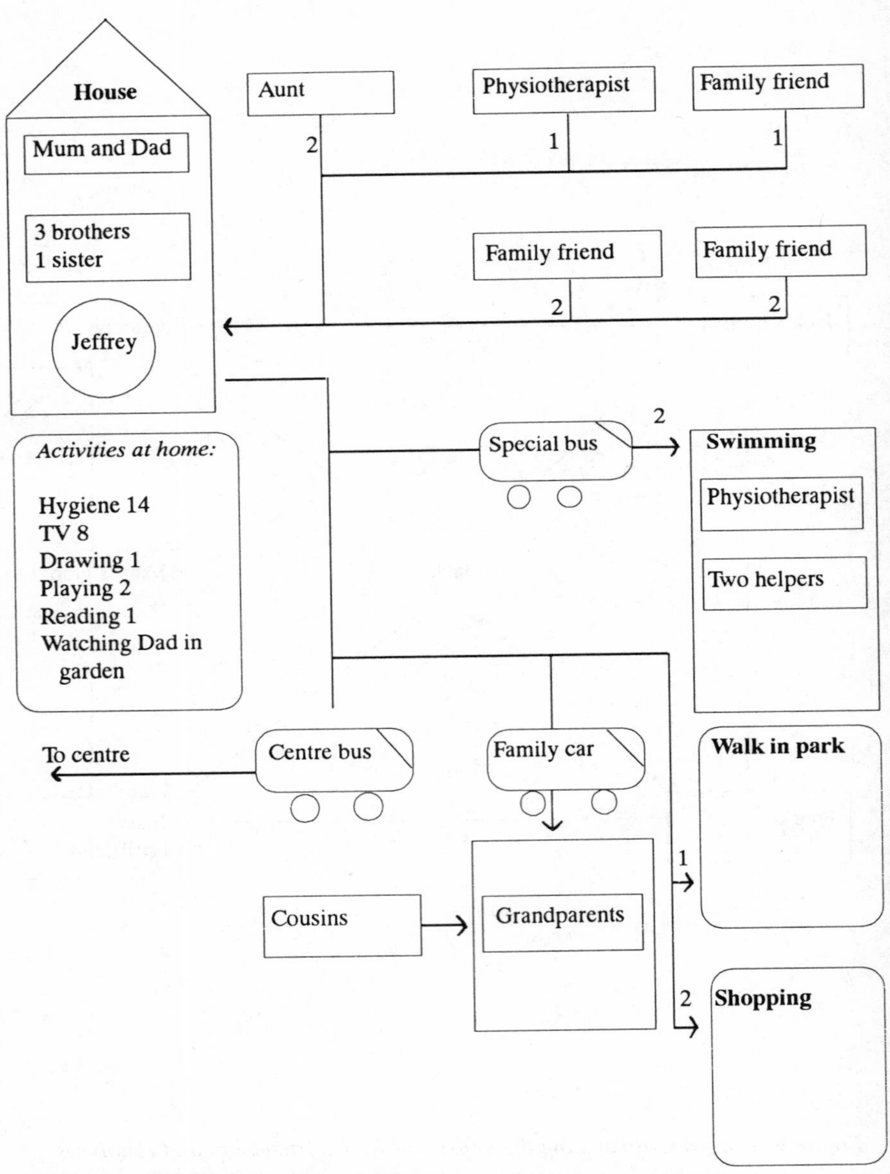

Figure 10: Jeffrey's home-based network

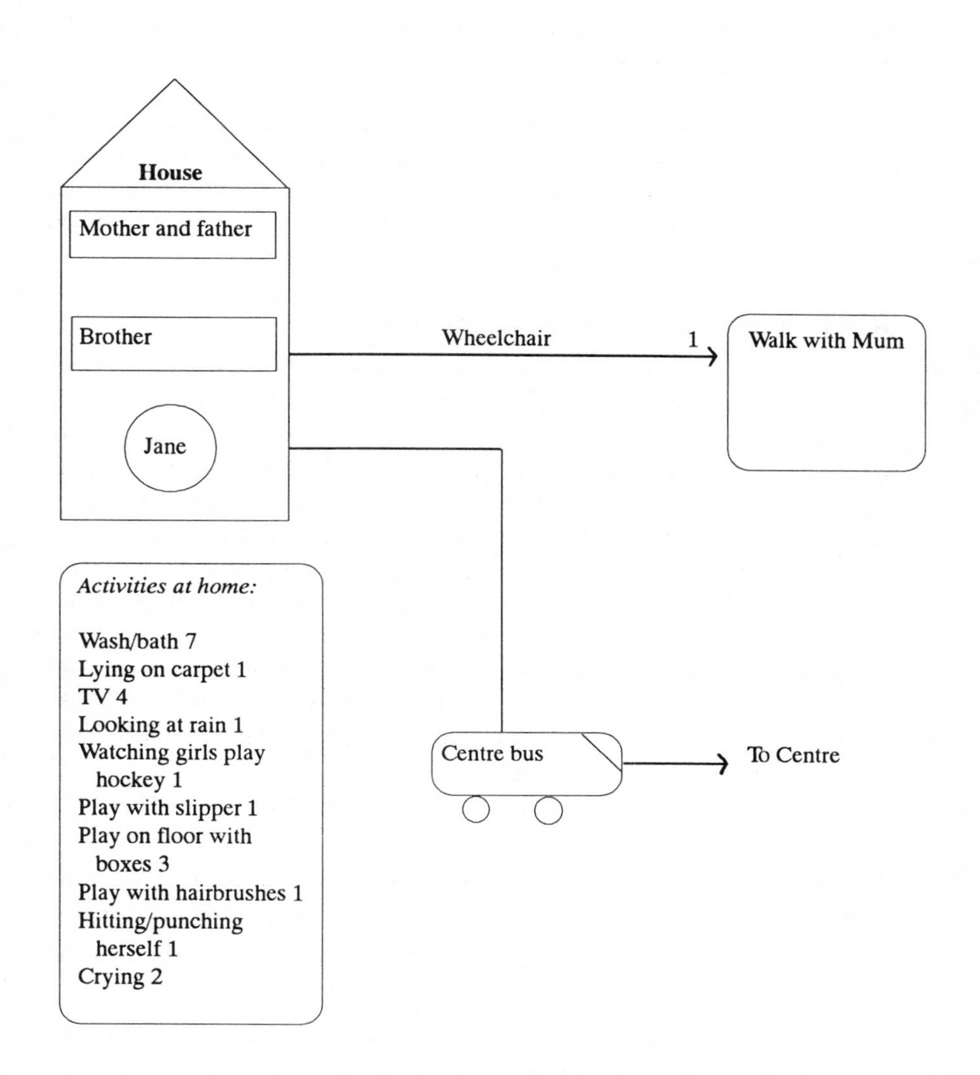

Figure 11: Jane's home-based network

Contrasting self-contained and embracing networks are illustrated in Figures 10 and 11, relating to young people with profound handicaps attending day centres. These examples are taken from *Case Studies for Practice 2*.

Both Jeffrey and Jane are wheelchair-bound, but what it means to be in a wheelchair presents a dramatic contrast. Jane's network is almost entirely restricted to attendance at the centre. She is closely bound up with her mother. Jeffrey's network, on the other hand, shows a life which is varied and it is hard to believe he is confined to a wheelchair.

Relational content (or relationship qualities)

Relational content is a technical term which would be used by sociologists. For social work purposes, it is perhaps simpler to talk about relationship qualities. So far we have spoken mainly about quantitative features of networks, i.e. how much contact there is between Jack and relations, friends and so on. Social workers will be particularly interested, not just in how much contact there is but in the quality of the relationships that Jack has with his mother, his brother and sister, his granny, his girlfriend and so on.

Network analysis takes us further than simply making judgemental statements about the quality of a particular relationship. The idea of relational content implies a descriptive analysis of different types of content. For example, a sociological text-book by Knoke and Kuklinski[1] suggests the following, based on a list of research topics: (reproduced by kind permission of the publishers, Sage).

(The language, including referring to people as 'actors' is more familiar to sociologists than to social workers!)

Transaction relations: actors exchange control over physical or symbolic media, for example, in gift giving or economic sales and purchases.

Communication relations: linkages between actors are channels by which messages may be transmitted from one actor to another.

Boundary penetration relations: the ties between actors consist of constituent sub-components held in common; for example, corporation boards of directors with overlapping members.

Instrumental relations: actors contact one another in efforts to secure valuable goods, services, or information, such as a job, an abortion, political advice, or recruitment to a social movement.

Sentiment relations: perhaps the most frequently investigated networks are those in which individuals express their feelings of affection, admiration, deference, loathing, or hostility towards each other.

Authority/power relations: these networks, usually occurring in complex formal organisations, indicate the rights and obligations of actors to issue and obey commands.

Kinship and descent relations: a special instance of several preceding generic type networks, these bonds indicate role relationships among family members.

Partly stimulated by this list, and partly based on the experience of colleagues in interpreting hundreds of different client networks, we have evolved the following classification of relationship qualities for network analysis in social work:

Communication and access. Here we are concerned with whether, in a particular relationship, the client gains access to other people and the opportunity to communicate with them. For example going back to Jack, for the second period of analysis (Figure 8) we may ask, does Jack's relationship with Fred enable Jack to meet other people at work and communicate with them?

Instrumental qualities. Here we are concerned with the ways in which the client's relationship with another person offers the client practical assistance or information which can be used in a practical way. For example, we might be concerned to understand to what extent Jack's girlfriend helps Jack in practical ways.

Sentiment qualities. Irrespective of whether Jack's girlfriend offers him practical help, we may be interested to know what kind of feelings or sentiments Jack has towards his girlfriend. Presumably he would say that he loves her but does this love contain elements of fear or respect or is anger an important component?

Influence. Here we are concerned with whether another person exercises a particular influence over the client. Again we could ask this in the example concerning Jack's girlfriend, with regard to Jack. Or perhaps we would be particularly interested to know what kind of influence, if any, Jack's granny exercises over him?

Esteem. This is a specific quality which we have included in the light of an increasing emphasis on the importance of our clients having a role in relation to others, which is respected and in keeping with the philosophy of what would broadly be called 'normalisation'. For example, does Jack's girlfriend esteem him in the sense of valuing him as an adult citizen? The opposite might be that she would see him as a delinquent who had to be reformed. Such an attitude would be one indicator of an absence of esteem.

Reciprocal qualities. Reciprocal qualities are the inversion of the other qualities, i.e. instead of asking what instrumental help Jack receives from others we ask in what ways Jack helps others instrumentally? Does he, for example, help his granny in practical ways, particularly since her accident? Does Jack provide the means of accessing his own friends so far as others are concerned? And so on.

Network features, network types and relationship qualities, therefore, represent different ways of reflecting upon and interpreting social networks. Earlier in this chapter I asked the reader to reflect on Jack's two networks. Perhaps some of your reflections are covered by the different kinds of appraisal we have suggested. There could be other ideas you might have in reflecting on Jack's network. For example, it is interesting to reflect on how little time Jack appears to spend at home. This could form the basis of a general question, which would come under the heading of network types, of how far the client is home-centred?. What is there at home for Jack? Other information components may help us to understand why he is so little home-centred. His father left home ten years ago but the mother had only recently re-married. Jack clearly feels literally 'put out' by the coming, not only of his new step-father, but of a new baby sister (which he always refers to as his half-sister). He does, however, maintain contact with his granny, and indeed granny shares with Jack a general disapproval of his step-father. Jack is a rather timid lad. He does not openly confront his step-father but simply spends as much time as possible away from home, initially with his mates in a cafe and more recently with his girlfriend. His girlfriend, who is a little older than himself, is able to offer him a sense of protection as well as the affection he lacks at home.

In summary, it can be said that social network analysis is all about making connections between different kinds of network features, types and relationship qualities. A classic example is provided in the research of one of the early pioneers in network analysis, Elizabeth Bott. As a result of studying a group of families she postulated a relationship between the degree of what she called 'conjugal segregation' and the pattern of relationships maintained by the partners' separate relationships with external people in their network. She also linked this with the degree of network density, i.e. the extent to which these 'external people' had relationships with one another. Subsequent evidence has sustained the hypothesis relating to dense social networks and segregated conjugal relationships. In other words, when the marriage partners tend separately to do their own thing at home, they each have their own close company of friends with whom they are in contact outside the homes.

The importance of Elizabeth Bott's findings lies not just in themselves but that they illustrated the potentiality of social network analysis in a way which is directly relevant to social work. For a long time social workers have been accustomed to analysing marital relationships. They have also traditionally paid some attention to friendships outside the home. Elizabeth Bott put the two together. In so doing, she demonstrated a method for understanding family dynamics in a community context. Curiously, her work received little attention in the mainstream of social work theory. Instead, her approach was taken up by sociologists and social anthropologists and it formed one of the starting points for the development of other applications of network analysis. But today, what with the increasing emphasis on neighbourhood, informal helping networks and understanding communities, and the wish to continue to understand family dynamics, the approach on which her work and subsequent work were based is increasingly relevant.

Two further points can be made at this stage about network analysis, with reference to other research and practice approaches. The first is that network analysis, as we have interpreted it, is characterised by an open-ended approach to the collection of information. Network features such as relations, friends, work-mates or whatever are classified from the data, through the network, after the information has been collected. In other words, we do not begin by asking clients to tell us who their friends are, which relations they are in contact with, and who their work mates are. Instead we ask them, firstly to keep diaries and then to refer, in an open-ended way, to the people, places and activities that are important. I believe there are some technical advantages in this approach which need not concern us here in detail. In general it can be said that an open-ended approach avoids such problems of definition as what constitutes a friend, compared with who constitutes a neighbour. It also allows clients freedom to put their own significance on particular relationships or events.

Secondly, social network analysis is based on evidence which is collected on a day-to-day basis by means of a diary kept by the client or by the main support person and others who may be key people. The method of keeping diaries and the open-ended approach go together. In the absence of diaries, one is forced to ask questions in terms of categories, e.g. can you name particular friends or relations or work-mates? The diary enables us to overstep such categorisation at this stage of data gathering. Afterwards we can then look at the networks with the clients and say, for example in Jack's case, who was Fred? The answer the client will give us will enable us to locate Fred in the work-place and not, say, the relatives' network.

This all seems very obvious to my colleagues who have been working with this approach for a number of years. But it has to be stated that it runs against a lot of conventional wisdom in social research. Part of the difficulty may be that researchers, as well as practitioners, sometimes lack confidence in using diary keeping as a technique for gathering information. How is it done? Is it reliable? We shall consider these and other questions of techniques in the next chapter.

Reference

1. Knoke, D., and Kuklinski, J., (1982), *Network Analysis*: Sage.

Discussion exercises

1. (Referred to in the text). Write down what strikes you about the type of network represented in Jack's case. Then compare what you have written with the discussion on page 38.

2. Consider the concept of 'density' in the networks of one or more of your clients. Who are the key people in the networks likely to be and how would you go about assessing the extent of the contacts between them? If you had the evidence, what use would this be for possible networking? (See Chapter 2).

3. Summarize the possible uses of network analysis for work with one or more of your clients, or client groups.

Chapter 4

Techniques

Clients are asked to record their patterns of daily living by means of a structured diary. Diaries for adult clients are usually kept for a fortnight. A week may be long enough for children or young people keeping their own diaries if the reliability or motivation would be likely to deteriorate after the first week. A week may also be sufficient if there is a very regular routine, e.g. a child attending school. On the other hand, a single week is often atypical and hence a fortnight is usually preferred. Sometimes, in the case of an elderly client living by themselves whose pattern of events is likely to be slow moving, a diary for a four week period may be considered.

A discovery over the past twelve years is that the large majority of clients easily become committed to keeping diaries, usually conscientiously and sometimes enthusiastically. Apart from the recording of pattern of daily living, the keeping of diaries sometimes helps clients to communicate and to learn to communicate. Some clients can express their feelings to a social worker more easily on paper than verbally.

When we say that diaries are structured we mean that the clients are not simply presented with a blank piece of paper or notebook. Some structure for the day is already suggested, based on our previous knowledge of what the client's daily structure is. For example, Figure 12 shows a suggested structured diary for use on days when a client is at work. Figure 13 shows a suggested structure for a diary for a client who is not at work but at home most of the day. The underlying principle of these diary formats is to enable clients to record the people, places and activities which are significant to them. Hence there is an emphasis on such questions as 'where did you go',

Agency/project

Diary for days at work

Diary for ______ (name) for ______ (day) ______ (dates)

	What happened? What did you do?	Who were you with?	Who did you meet?
Before work			
At work			
After work			

How did you travel to and from work? ______

Did anything happen on these journeys? ______

Figure 12: A structured diary format for a day at work

Agency/project

Diary for days at work

Diary for __________ (name) for __________ (day) __________ (dates)

	What happened? What did you do?	**Who were you with?**	**Who did you meet?**
Morning			
Lunch-time			
Afternoon			
Evening (night)			

What journeys did you make from home?

To:	*How did you travel?*	*Who were you with?*	*Who did you meet?*

Add comments on the back of this sheet if you wish: e.g. if the day was very unusual. If anyone helped you complete the diary, their comments are also welcome.

Figure 13: A structured diary format for a day at home

Hospital diary for ______________ **(name) for** ______________ **(day)** ______________ **(date)**

'Where were you today?' List events or activities while you were:			Who were you with? *(If lots of people, name up to five who were most important. Explain who they are (e.g. patient/nurse/doctor/relation/friendetc.))*
	(a) in the ward	(b) elsewhere in hospital	Name: *(Who they are)*
1. During the morning			
2. Lunch-time			
3. During the afternoon			
4. During the evening or night			

(c) Did you go outside the hospital today? Tick: *all day/ morning / lunch-time / afternoon / evening / overnight*

Places visited	Who with?	How did you travel?	Event or activity	Who else did you meet?

Extent of assistance: Tick: *written by patient / dictated by patient / written by staff in discussion with patient / completed by staff without help from patient*

Additional comments from person(s) who assisted in completing diary for today: *(Continue overleaf if necessary. Include supplementary information if you think diary is not otherwise complete)*

Figure 14: A structured diary format for a day in hospital 'who were you with', 'what did you do'. Note that we are also interested in how people travel including whom they meet on journeys.

Figure 14 is a suggested diary format for the client in hospital. Here a distinction is made between activities within the ward and activities that are outside the ward but still within the hospital.

Figure 15 (page 54) shows a suggested diary format for a child or young person in a residential setting. In this case the structure is kept as simple as possible.

Note that in all the diary formats there is an opportunity for clients to express comments. Clients will vary enormously in the extent to which they will do this. Some will give one- or two-word answers for each section of the day while others will want to write on the back of the diary forms as well as on the front! Even a diary which is minimally filled up can still contain enough information to enable us to draw an accurate network for a fortnight (or whatever period has been chosen) in the client's life.

There could be variations in these four basic diary structures. For example, in a diary format for an elderly person in a residential setting, it may be useful to distinguish between activities pursued in the client's own room and activities in the communal part of the building.

It is important that clients are asked, and not told, to keep diaries for whatever purpose they are being kept. It is useful to say what this purpose is. For example, in the case of a client who is in a long-stay hospital awaiting discharge to a community, it can be explained that it will be helpful to have a picture of the client's daily routine, special events and special interests in order to consider with them where they might wish to live in the community and what support will be required. If the purpose of keeping diaries is for staff training or research purposes this also should be stated. In the series *Case Studies for Practice*, which is designed mainly for staff training purposes, clients' permission is always sought and, so far, there have been no refusals.

For social workers who are in regular contacts with their clients, it is not necessary to programme additional visits. If the social worker happens to be visiting for other reasons during the period when the diaries are kept - what we call the 'monitored period' - the client can be asked about his progress in keeping the diaries and if there have been any difficulties. Sometimes a mid-monitoring visit is important. If this is not the case, however, the diary forms may be left with the client on a previous visit making it clear on which day the diary keeping is to start. The social worker's phone number can be given in case there are any difficulties and the diaries will be collected after completion of the monitored period.

The standard diary formats we have shown in Figures 12-15 are on the basis of a new page (or in the case of the child in a residential setting, a folder) for each day. Sheets are stapled together for the proposed monitored fortnight with variations in the format as appropriate for different days. For example, for the fortnight for a client normally at work five days a week, a bundle of diary forms would be prepared consisting of five formats for days at work followed by two for days at home at the weekend, another five for the next week at work and two, finally, for the last two days at home. A spare page or two can be added. These diary forms are then provided with a folder or large envelope.

Sometimes clients will need help from others in keeping their diaries. This does not invalidate the diary. We refer to the person who offers help as the 'support person' and if this is the same person who offers the main support in daily living generally, he or she will be called the 'main support person'. The two are likely to be one and the same but they could be different. For example, in the case of an adult learning to read or write, the support person, for diary purposes, could well be the adult literacy tutor and, in this case, the keeping of a diary would be part of the tuition programme. More frequently the support person for the diary will be the main support person at home, such as mother or father in the case of a young person or a person with complex learning difficulties, and perhaps a son or daughter or other relation in the case of an elderly person living at home. In the case of a single person, for example in sheltered housing, the main support person could be another resident or conceivably the warden. Occasionally the diary support person might be a visiting professional.

Where a diary is kept with support from another person it is important to know the extent of the support. The diary support person will always be asked to ensure that, as far as possible, it is the client's own diary and not theirs. We therefore need to know which of the following applies:

- Daily diary kept by client himself with support from X.
- Daily diary dictated by client but written by X.
- Daily diary written by X with client's participation.

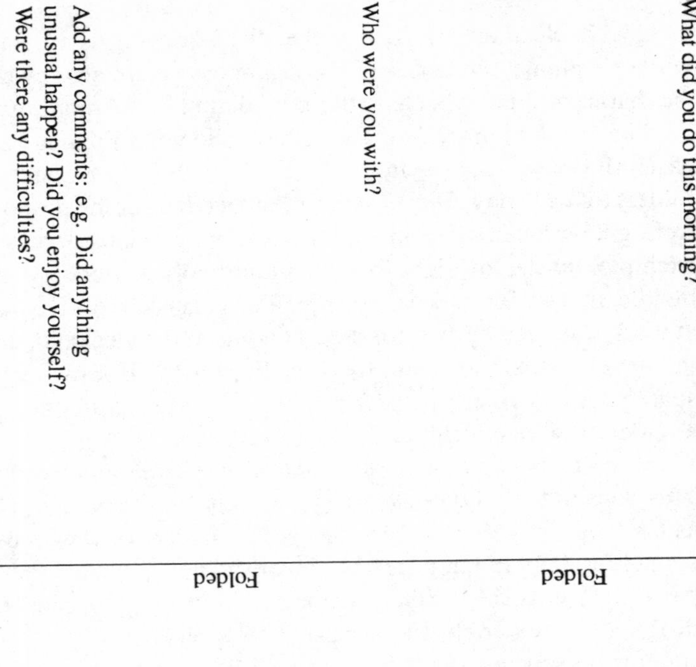

Figure 15: Format for a child's diary kept at a residential school

Daily diary

Kept by ____________________

with support from ____________

for __________ (day) __________ (date)

Folded

What did you do this evening?

Who were you with?

Add any comments: e.g. Did anything unusual happen? Did you enjoy yourself? Were there any difficulties?

Part four
(practitioner version)

Social network analysis
Follow-up discussion of diaries

Procedure:
When diaries are completed, the social worker/researcher will visit the client to discuss the most important people, places and activities that featured in the diaries. If a main support person helped the client keep the diaries it will be useful if they are also present for this interview.

We are interested in what went on outside the home and in the community, and the part played by relations, friends, volunteers, officials and so on in connection with the client's activities and visits etc. Social work staff will only be included as important people if they featured outside their official duties.

Firstly, ask if we can go through the diaries, picking out the (three) most important activities (outside the home).

Activity	Where held	Who with *	Why was it important?
1.			
2.			
3.			

* Under 'Who with?' indicate the size and composition of the group.

Secondly, ask who are the most important people named in the diary. (These people could be included in those listed above under activities or other people). *Exclude people living in client's household and also exclude social worker interviewing client.*

Person	Relationship to client (e.g. relative, friend, shopkeeper, Minister, etc. etc.)
1.	
2.	
3.	

Figure 16: Format for diary follow-up

Now, for each of the three named people, ask the following questions:

Question 1 *(Communication and access qualities)*

Does ______________ make it possible for you to meet other people you would not otherwise meet? (Explore answer in terms of how the relationship helps the client in communication with others).

Question 2 *(Instrumental qualities)*

Does ______________ help you in practical ways? (e.g. practical tasks or, perhaps, simply giving information to the client).

Question 3 *(Sentiments)*

Apart from whether ______________ helps you in practical ways, how do you feel towards him/her? (e.g. affection, friendliness, respect, anger, resentment - or perhaps no feeling at all?)

Question 4 *(Influence)*

To what extent does ______________ exercise influence over you? What kind of influence? (e.g. helpful/unhelpful)

Question 5 *(Esteem)*

Would you say ______________ shows that he/she values you as a person as he/she would his/her (other) friends?

Give an example.

Question 6 *(Reciprocal qualities)*

Finally, what does ______________ gain from the relationship with you? What kind of things do you do for him/her?

- Daily diary kept by X without client's participation.

A front sheet with these options can be added to a bundle of diaries presented to the client and the support person can indicate which most closely applies.

When the social worker returns to pick up the diaries any uncertainties, omissions or ambiguities can be clarified. In particular, it is important to go through the diaries identifying who the particular people who have been mentioned are. For example, who is Fred? Is he a friend or a relation? Who is Peter? Is it the same Peter who is a member of the household? The social worker can add clarifying comments to the diary forms, perhaps with a different coloured pen or pencil.

After doing this, it is often a good opportunity to undertake what we call the diary follow up. Part of the standard format for this schedule is shown in Figures 16. The social worker begins, after looking at the diaries, by asking the client for information about the three most important places or activities - places they go to and things they do - either shown in the diaries or, if there was some particular reason why they were not included in the diaries, why this should be. Clients are asked to name up to three significant places or activities outside their own homes. We also usually exclude social work facilities such as a day centre or visits to the social worker. Clients do not *have* to name just three but we do not want a long list of thirty three! Selecting three puts an emphasis on the most important or significant. We have had very few problems with clients in giving answers to this particular question. We then go on to ask why each place or activity is important and, here again, clients can usually give a straightforward and illuminative answer. For example:

Why is the Ace Club particularly important to you?

- *Because it is the only time I get to go out and meet people.*

We move on from significant places and activities to ask questions about the three most important people in the client's life. Again, the client can name persons not included in the diary, but in this case the social worker will want to ask why they do not appear in the diary and perhaps check with the client that they are persons that are important now and not simply in the past. There may be a perfectly good reason why they do not feature in the diary - perhaps they were on holiday, for example. Importance is not necessarily signified by daily or weekly contacts. However, since we are concentrating on patterns of daily living we are not particularly interested, for this purpose, in people who may only be seen on very rare occasions, however much store is attached to the people concerned. If none of the three suggested people feature in the diary we might be suspicious either that the diaries had not been kept accurately or that some of the named people belonged to a past life rather than to the present.

Note that the follow-up schedule, like other schedules used, is completed by the social worker with the client and sometimes with the main support person or diary support person also present. The role of the support person is to help interpret what the client is saying. It is not, or should not be, to impose their own views.

Exceptionally, a social worker may feel that a schedule such as the follow-up schedule can be left for the client to complete himself or herself and forwarded by post. Where we have tried this with particular clients it has usually been successful.

The questions themselves in this schedule are self-explanatory and the reasons for their inclusion were discussed in Chapter 3. In a schedule, as distinct from a questionnaire, the form in which the question is put is not of over-riding importance so long as the correct sense of the question is conveyed. The form of words used will thus vary according to the form of words which would appear natural both to the social worker to speak and for the client to understand. My experience is that clients grasp the essence of each of these relationship qualities very quickly. Perhaps the two hardest ones are the questions relating to sentiment and esteem. It is sometimes difficult for clients to express feelings about their personal relationships on the spur of the moment in response to questions that are posed. Time must therefore be given for the question to sink in and for the client to add comments after his or her first response. The question about esteem is difficult because esteem is not a word that many clients will use. Whatever words are appropriate we have to convey to the client that we are interested in whether the person we are considering shows respect for them as a normal person and values the relationship as they would a relationship with any other of their friends, and not as somebody who is in some way different or inferior.

Other schedules

While the diary and the follow up are perhaps the most unfamiliar parts of the network analysis information gathering process, other information is also important. Other schedules will normally be combined in a single sheaf of papers (see Appendix) and included with the schedule for the diary follow-up. The order in which they are completed is not important and will vary according to the social worker's discretion and skill. I find that I usually start with the social setting and social background. Much of this will already be known to the social worker and it will only be a question of updating and confirming that it is correct.

The features of performance schedule is a slightly more difficult exercise. If we are meeting a client for the first time, or, at least before we know them very well, it is useful to complete this schedule early on to get a clear picture of whom we are talking about. I say 'of whom we are talking about' because this schedule will sometimes be completed by the main support person instead of the client himself or herself (or in the presence of the main support person who can corroborate the answers). This particularly applies to someone who has physical or learning difficulties but in general the features of performance schedule is about living with other people and the key person one lives with is, in this sense, the key witness. We find, therefore, that the features of performance schedule is usually completed with the main support person, the exception being when a client who is living alone. Even in this case, if for example a person is elderly, a home help may be an appropriate person to assist and validate the answers.

The schedule is divided into three parts (see Appendix). The first part concerns self management skills such as dressing, washing, communicating and so on. These are the basic tasks, the performance of which constitutes personal autonomy. The second part concerns daily living skills and the third part concerns social skills.

The schedule is designed in such a way that if, as with many clients, there are no self management problems, the numeral '1' can be circled in each area of skill. No more questions have to be asked. In other words, one can skim through the schedule very quickly until we come to a group of questions where there are difficulties. We then pause to consider the reasons. For example, the question of using public transport may bring out difficulties which could relate to a lack of understanding of how to use money or, perhaps, a fear of going out alone. Again, however, if there were no issues or problems the numeral '1' is circled and one moves on to the next question.

Where the answer is not '1', in other words where there are difficulties or issues to be discussed, a series of prompts are suggested. These can be varied to suit the circumstances. The point of the exercise is to discover what the issues are in this particular area of functioning, what assistance or support is needed and the implications for staffing or equipment.

The schedule explains that a distinction is made between 'support' and 'assistance'. Assistance is taken to mean actual, physical help whereas support refers to encouragement, supervision or other non-physical forms of help.

Notes are also made throughout the schedule of progress that has been made and normally we take this to mean progress during the past year. There is also space to note the staffing and equipment implications of performing particular tasks or skills. These may form the basis of a client-needs approach to planning a future service (see Chapter 9).

Towards the end of the schedule, there are questions on social learning and a summary confirming progress or the lack of progress in home management, recreational activities, social activities in mixing with others, basic education, communicating with others and general confidence. This is followed by an open-ended question as to whether there is anything specific that the client has learnt - whatever it is - during the past year. This could be anything from learning to cross the road to gaining confidence in speaking to people.

The final question in this schedule asks whether there has been not only a lack of progress but regression in some respect.

The various 'views' schedules, as we call them, can be completed as opportunity arises either before or after the completion of the diaries. It perhaps makes more sense to complete them afterwards because some of the questions relate to the client's, and other people's, views about activities which are undertaken and which will have been referred to in the diaries. It will be noted that almost identical questions are asked in finding out the views of the different people we are concerned with. (See Appendix). These are the client himself or herself, the main support person and also the views of the social worker or other professional person involved.

Having collected all the information, the next step is to draw the networks from the diaries. In doing this, one will sometimes need to refer to basic information in the other schedules for confirmation - for example confirmation as to which people mentioned in the diary live at home.

It is my usual practice to draw a rough sketch of a diary to begin with. I go through each day and draw the appropriate symbol and add the appropriate words to it. For example, if on Monday Mrs Jones went to the local shops by herself, did her housework, watched TV and in the evening had a visit from Joe Bloggs this will be drawn as shown below (Figure 17).

If on Tuesday, Mrs Jones went to the Bank and had another visit from Joe Bloggs I would add these. I would indicate a second visit from Joe Bloggs with a tick and after completing the draft of the network for all 14 days I would add up the number of ticks and substitute for these a numeral.

There are various techniques for completing the final presentation of network drawings. It is possible to get your stationer to produce a set of rubber stamps to draw the key symbols quickly. Alternatively, we now use peel-off stickers which a printer can provide. A sheet of stickers is usually sufficient for each network drawing and costs (at the time of writing) about 10p. This method is used for the reproduction of drawings in this book. Alternatively, some social workers will prefer to draw their diagrams individually by hand with a pencil and ruler.

We like to give attention to standardised layouts. This enables us to pick out network features quickly when we are looking at a series of diagrams. The following are the main conventions:

- Place the client's home in the top left corner.
- Place the client's main occupation base in the bottom left corner.
- Visits in (which we sometimes call 'lines in') from the top right corner.
- Visits out from home - middle-right of sheet.
- Visits out from occupation base - bottom-right.

Sometimes a network is too large to go on a single sheet. It can conveniently be divided between a home-based section and an occupation-based section (i.e. between a home-based network and a work-based or centre-based network). Alternatively, if the family go on holiday during a monitored fortnight it may be useful to display the holiday based network on a separate sheet. In each case, however, where separate sheets are used the lines which connect up the network as a whole need to be shown. For example, a line

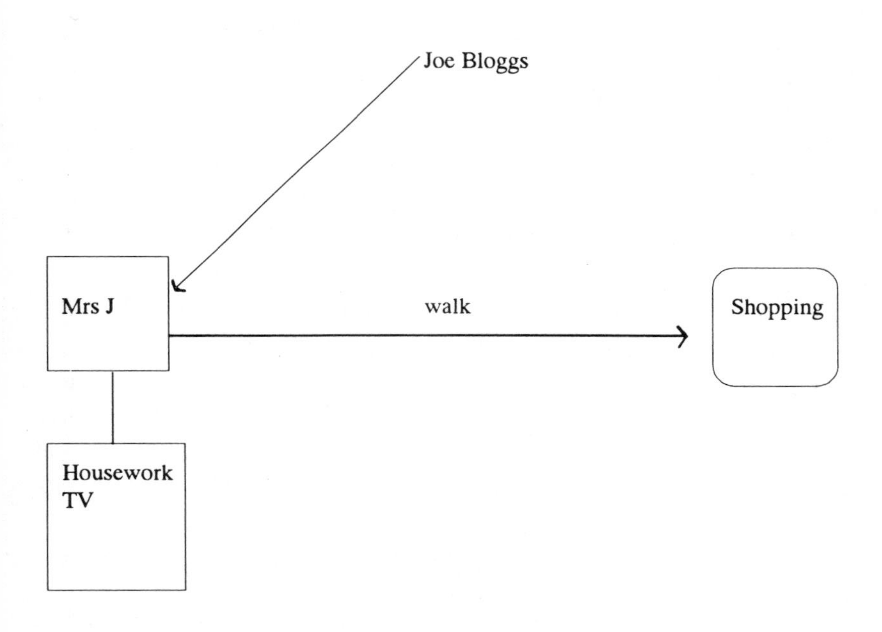

Figure 17: Starting to draw a rough sketch of a network based on Day 1 of Mrs J's diary

leading from home to the bottom of the page will indicate 'to work place' (or whatever).

What do we do with information from the schedules? If it is simply for individual case records, it may be useful to write a short summary. If however, information is being collected for monitoring purposes over a period of time and involving many other clients, the codes which are provided in the schedules may be used for the entry of the data into a computer. (See Chapter 9).

Without such a large-scale exercise as this, however, we may be interested to compare the networks for groups of clients on our case load, and over a period of time. For this purpose we use a number of concepts derived from more theoretical applications of network analysis. The main ones are the following:

Lines in - this refers to the number of lines appearing in the network drawing which come to the client at home or at work from elsewhere.

Lines out - this refers to all lines that appear in the network going outwards from the client at home or at work to other people, places or activities outside. (N.B.: where a line is both 'in' and 'out', i.e. if the client both visits the person and is visited by them, this counts both as a line 'in' and as a line 'out'.)

Intensity - this term is used to refer to the number of lines in and out multiplied by their occurrence during the monitored period. It can be used as a rough and ready indicator of the extensiveness of a client's network. For example, an intensity score of under 5 (for a fortnight) would be very low and a score of over 20 would be quite extensive.

The difference between 'lines in' and 'lines out' may be interesting in indicating the extent to which a client is more likely to receive visitors at home than to go out to meet friends or other contacts elsewhere. We have found, for example, that it is a feature of people with learning difficulties living at home that they usually have more visits or lines out than visits or lines in.

A further term which is sometimes used is *duration*. This is only relevant if the diary format has allowed us to record the length of time the client was involved in making particular contacts. We have used this format but we have not found it worthwhile including it for social work practitioner, as distinct from research, usage.

Discussion exercises

1. What would be the most appropriate diary format for your work. Consider any modifications that might be helpful.

2. Practice drawing a network from your first completed diary. Add up the lines 'in' and 'out' and work out the intensity score.

3. Practice completing the schedules contained in the Appendix. Reflect on the order in which you find it most helpful to ask the questions. Note any questions which are particularly important for your work.

4. Consider the most appropriate length of time for diary keeping for the clients you are working with, i.e. a week, a fortnight or longer.

5. Practice various ways of asking questions, or offering cues, to clients - especially with regard to the diary follow-up when questions are asked about relationship qualities.

6. Practice completing the features of performance schedule. (See Appendix).

Part Two

Applications

Chapter 5

Field work assessments and reviews

Network analysis can form the framework for social work assessments and reviews, including individualised needs-led assessments envisaged in the new legislation in Britain concerned with 'Care in the Community'. It also has a wider application in field social work, including child care.

We consider this under two headings:

1. Referrals to the key field social worker (or case manager) for a holistic assessment.
2. Referrals on from a social worker, or case manager, for specific services.

Referrals to the field social worker

The referral process can be represented graphically in the form of a network drawing. This is useful both in enabling the social worker to reflect on the significance to the client of the referral process and in providing a ready means of recalling the referral circumstances for future reference. We use the standard network symbols with the additional symbol of a diamond shape to represent 'intermediaries' in the referral process. Figure 18 shows a referral network in which a client referred herself to a social worker, but where a General Practitioner and the health visitor could be described as intermediaries. This case was a self-referral in the sense that the client took the initiative and went to see the social worker at her social work office. However, it is important to record what happened before that event. This is a record of what happened:

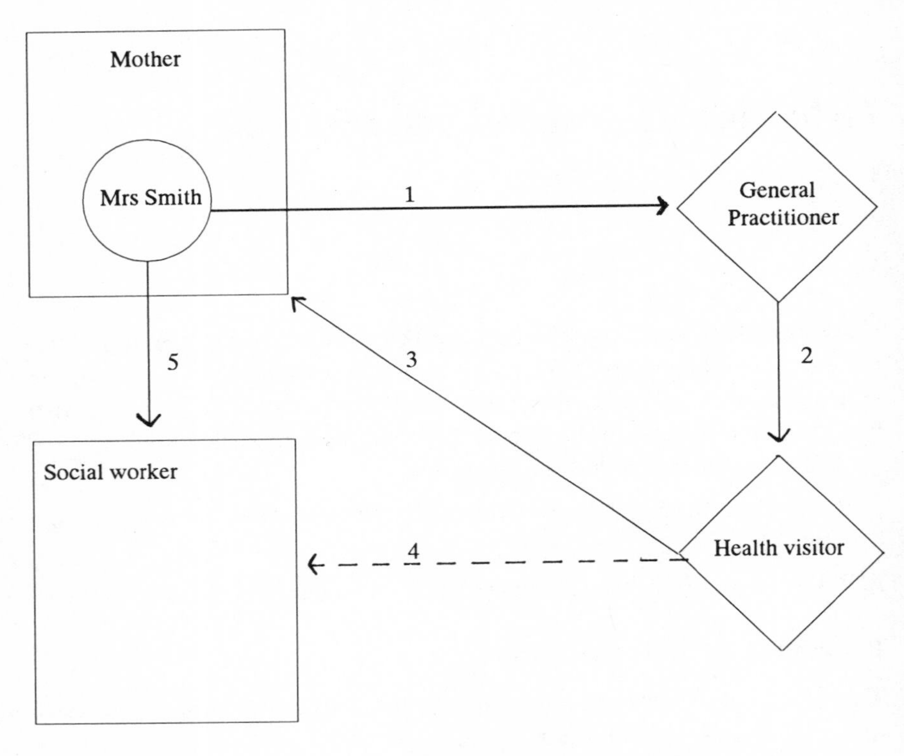

Key: Personal contacts ⟶
Telephone contacts – – – →
Sequence of contacts indicated by numbers

Intermediary contacts shown with diamonds

Figure 18: Referral network - self-referral of a client to a social worker with general practitioner and health visitor as intermediaries.

> Mrs Smith, aged 55, lives with her invalid mother. She has reached a state of acute anxiety because she cannot cope with her mother's bizarre behaviour and yet she feels it is not right to allow her mother to go into an old people's home. A month before the referral, Mrs Smith went to see her G.P., complaining of nerves. The G.P. realised there was a social dimension to Mrs Smith's problem and referred it to the health visitor at the same health centre. The health visitor then visited Mrs Smith. After discussing her problems with her, she thought that Mrs Smith should see a social worker. Mrs Smith was unfamiliar with social workers and the health visitor felt that to prepare the way she should contact the social work office to ask for a visit. In discussion, however, the social worker asked the health visitor to ask Mrs Smith if she was willing to take the initiative to see the social worker at the social work office. This was partly because Mrs Smith was quite able to get out and about and her mother could be left alone during the daytime. It was also because the social worker thought that, in this case, it would be better to talk to Mrs Smith without her mother being present in the first instance. Mrs Smith agreed and so presented herself at the social work office, technically as a self-referral.

Perhaps it is arguable that since the health visitor had contacted the social worker, it could be regarded as a referral from the health visitor. The point we are making, however, is that any referral is not a single event but is part of a referral process in which a number of people are likely to be involved. No client wakes up one morning and entirely out of the blue, without prompting from anyone, says 'I will go and see the social worker'. This would at least be unlikely. Someone would have suggested the idea. Similarly, the person who is apparently the referring person will, in turn, have been prompted by someone else. In this case, in so far as the health visitor was the referring person, she had been prompted to do so by the G.P. who, in turn, had been prompted by Mrs Smith herself. The network analysis procedures help us to see the referral process for what it is - not a single act or event, but a sequence of events involving a number of different people and agencies. We can present this in the form of the network drawing shown in Figure 18.

Let us take another example, which is more complicated than the example of Mrs Smith. Readers in England and Wales or elsewhere outside

Scotland will forgive me for taking an example from the Scottish system of children's hearings. This takes the place of care proceedings involving juvenile courts in England and Wales.

> Tom had been in trouble for stealing on his way home from school. At first it was frivolous, like stealing apples from an elderly person's garden. As it persisted, however, and after many complaints, it became more serious, involving pilfering from parked cars. After various warnings to Tom, the police decided to refer him to the Reporter to the children's panel. The Reporter's job is to consider, in the light of reports requested from the Social Work and Education Departments, whether or not 'compulsory measures of care' are needed. If this is seen to be the case, Tom and his parents are ordered, as a legal requirement, to appear before a Children's Hearing. The initial referral, therefore, so far as the social worker was concerned, was in the form of a letter received by the social work office from the Children's Panel Reporter. The social worker then visited the home. In this case the parents were concerned about their child and readily attended the Hearing. The social worker recommended to the Hearing that Tom be placed on supervision since it did not appear to be a situation which justified more drastic measures. The school also prepared a report after consulting the educational psychologist to see if they had previous information and what their view would be about recommending to the hearing that Tom be assessed.

In many Hearings, a great many other people would also be involved but this is complicated enough! Figure 19 represents in diagrammatic form exactly what happened during this complex referral process.

In both Mrs Smith's and Tom's case the information we have gained about the referral process represents a useful background sheet for the assessment itself.

The assessment will require many, if not all, of the components of the network analysis exercise described in the first part of this book. Social workers will be familiar with the idea of social history and they will also be familiar with the idea of including basic information about the social setting. The difference is that these things are now incorporated in a more focused and structured analysis of the part that the social worker and others will play *in the context of the client's pattern of daily living*. Network

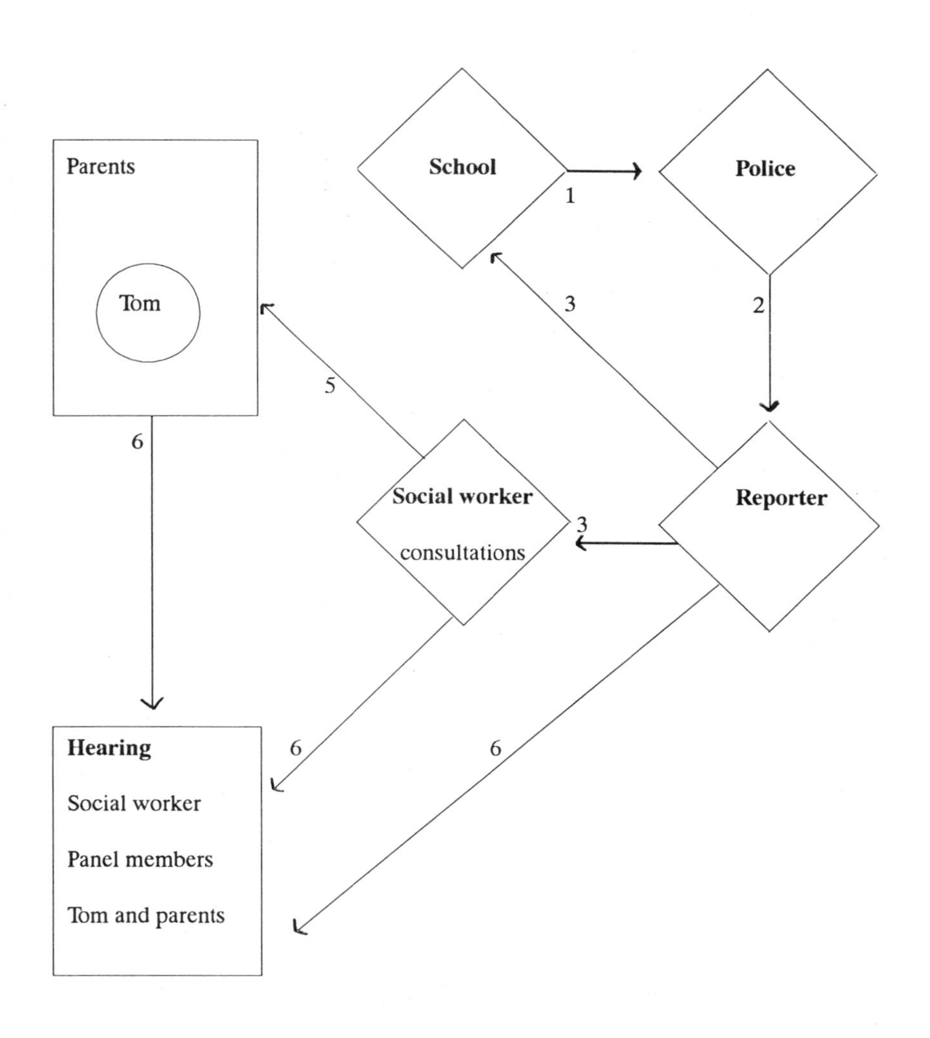

Figure 19: Referral of a child to a Children's Hearing in Scotland - Tom

analysis will also ensure that the views of the client himself or herself as well as the views of the main support person to the client, come to the fore.

Network analysis enables us either to focus on the presenting client or to move away from the presenting client and examine the social network more generally. Others within the network may also be in need of social work attention. For example, in Mrs Smith's case, the social worker may well decide that it is really Mrs Smith's mother who needs attention. Indeed, in one sense, Mrs Smith herself can be regarded as part of the referral process since although she presented herself to her G.P. suffering from nerves, in coming to the social worker she recognised that the cause of her 'nerves' was that she did not know how to help and deal with her mother at home. Who, then, is the client? Is it Mrs Smith or Mrs Smith's mother? In this particular case, the network analysis approach would most obviously offer the suggestion that the mother should be regarded as the client and Mrs Smith should be regarded as the main support person. Expressed in other terms, Mrs Smith is an informal carer and her mother is the person cared for. Network analysis helps us to see this more clearly. The social worker pursuing the network analysis approach would discuss with Mrs Smith the feasibility of keeping a diary, with the mother's co-operation, of the mother's daily life over a period of, say, a fortnight. There would then be a systematic consideration either of what steps could be taken to make the mother's life more fulfilling from her home base or, if this is totally impossible, whether life would offer substantially more in a sheltered or residential setting. Opportunities for Mrs Smith to enrich her own life may help to ease the burden of caring.

It may, of course, transpire that Mrs Smith, the original presenting client, has anxieties of her own which do not entirely spring from her concern for her mother. But the social worker should not assume that this possibility is the first avenue to pursue with Mrs Smith. Were it nevertheless to transpire that this was the case, then it would be important to consider Mrs Smith's pattern of daily living as well as the mother's. It would first be necessary to identify with Mrs Smith if there was anyone in her life whom she would regard as her main support person. Would it, for example, in spite of the difficulties, be her mother? Were there other people she could turn to? A daily diary kept by Mrs Smith would help to reveal the answers to these questions both for Mrs Smith's benefit and to enable the social worker to see more clearly where the focus of work should be.

In households where two members equally constitute a social work client, it is better initially to draw two separate networks, one for each person concerned, compatible with a family carework approach. As a more sophisticated exercise in network analysis, a single drawing could be used, with perhaps the separate contacts of each client drawn using a different coloured pen.

Let us assume that this has been accomplished with the two members of the Smith household. The following are the sort of features that might be revealed:

> Mother is hesitant to get out and meet friends although she does, in fact, have people who take an interest in her and would only be too glad to become more involved if she would allow them to do so.
>
> Mother needs to lead a life of her own, independent of her attempt to continue to play the role of mother at home to her daughter.
>
> When this fails, mother adopts the role of being a child to her daughter.

Social network analysis will also help to give a clearer picture of Tom's daily living situation. His father is away from home a lot with his work. It transpires that his mother, as well as his older sister, recently started full-time work when the latter left school. These factors make Tom's passage through adolescence a lonely experience. He has few friends at school and few outside interests. As in the Smith case, there is some merit in the exercise of network analysis helping the social worker to identify who is the main support person in his life. The keeping of diaries was, in this case, initially resisted by the parents. Eventually, Tom kept his own diary with help from his mother. This act in itself helped the mother to take a closer interest in Tom's life, instead of feeling guilt or anger. The keeping of diaries was also a therapeutic experience for Tom, helping him to express his feelings about everyday life.

Referrals from a field social worker to others

A social worker may sometimes refer a client to someone within his or her existing network. One of the benefits of keeping records based on a network analysis approach involving client diaries is that such people can more easily be identified. This applies particularly, for example, when a period of statutory supervision is coming to an end. It may be known that within a client's network there already exists another professional person, or perhaps a volunteer, who can incorporate some of the particular responsibilities which the social worker was fulfilling and which need not necessarily come to an abrupt end when the supervision or other statutory requirement is completed.

Sometimes, however, a referral to some new agency or facility is required just because it is not available within the existing network. Consider for example, the position of Mrs Smith's mother, discussed earlier. One of the options available to the social worker, in consultation with Mrs Smith as the mother's main support person and, of course, with the mother herself, would be a day centre. However, a referral to a day centre should be based on a thorough understanding of the precise way in which it is going to augment Mrs Smith's mother's network of friends. We may also, of course, consider the effect such a referral will have upon Mrs Smith herself. We have already said that Mrs Smith was not necessarily tied to her mother throughout the day. In fact, her main problems were during the evening and night when the mother was more prone to becoming over-active and a source of anxiety. Nevertheless, it was felt that attendance at a day centre would help the mother to develop a life of her own outside the house and that this would indirectly help her to be a calmer person in her life as a whole. This in turn, would help Mrs Smith to be calmer. In this case, it was helpful to pass on to the respective day centre a complete picture of the mother's life, based on a diary which had been kept for fourteen days. This also meant that it was possible to compare Mrs Smith's life and the life of her mother both prior to the referral to the day centre and, for example, three months later.

To make these procedures easier, it is possible to devise a standard assessment form incorporating network analysis. A suggested format is shown in Figure 20. The first page of the form covers the client's personal information and social setting. The second page contains a format for a sketch of the client's social network. It can be substituted for an actual network drawing where diaries have been kept, but in any situation where diaries have not been kept, a network can be simplified to contain information based on the client's responses to the questions concerning the most significant people, places and activities outside the home in daily living. It also contains information about the client's occupation; the term 'occupation' is taken to cover work, work experience and attendance at a day centre,

Page One

Agency:

Regarding: *(Name of client)*

Personal information and social setting:

Address and telephone:

Description of accommodation:

Description of neighbourhood:

Proximity and access to amenities and services:

Disability/health problems or issues:

Social/behavioural problems or issues:

Client's history (as relevant):
(a) schooling

(b) residential placements

(c) occupational history (including adult education) since leaving school:

Figure 20a: Assessment form (page one)

Pattern of daily living: draw lines to/from home to indicate important contacts. Add along lines usual frequency of contacts e.g. (weekly), (monthly) etc.

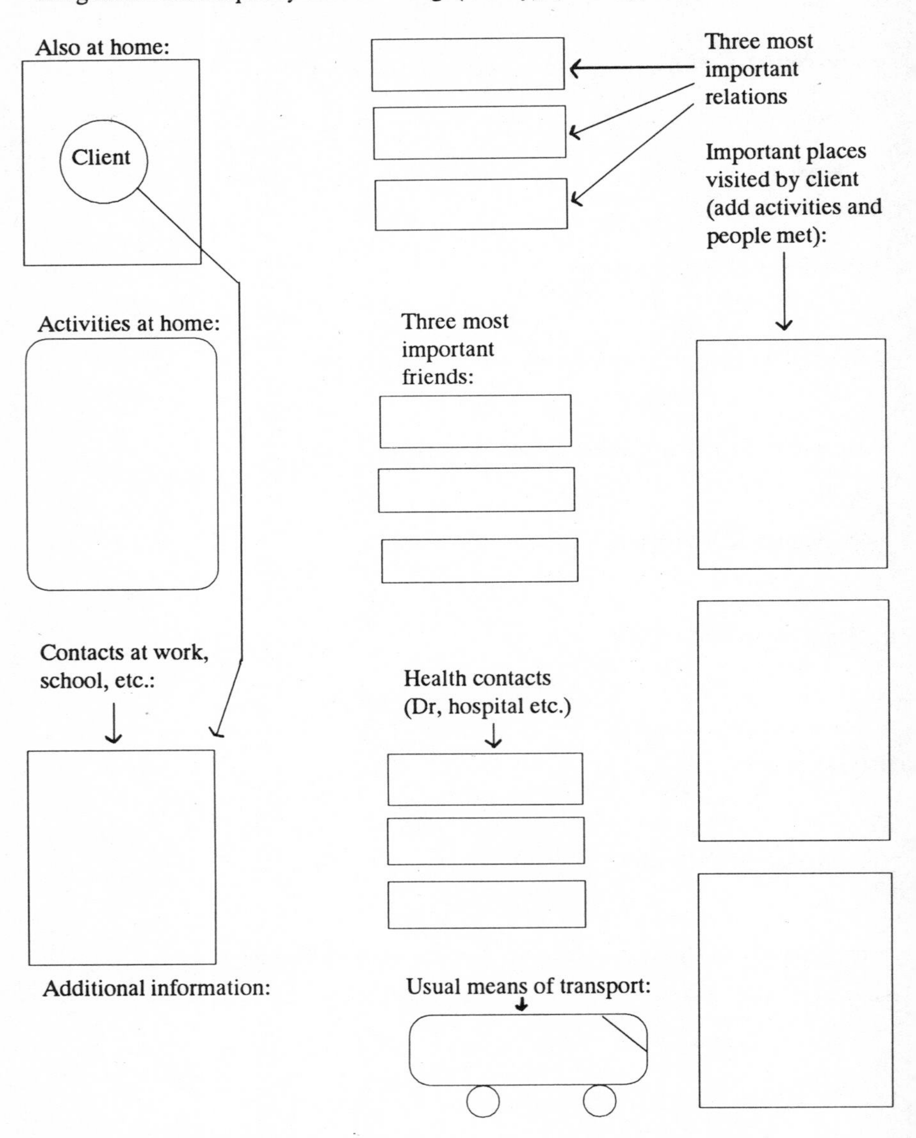

Figure 20b: Page two

Page Three

Features of client's performance

Indicate the level of support/assistance required (if any) for:

Self-management activities *(e.g. dressing, washing, toilet, mobility, basic communication):*

Daily living activities *(e.g. travel, busses, managing money, domestic, cooking etc.):*

Social activities and social interaction with others:

Special interests (a) indoor and (b) outdoor:

In what ways (if at all) are any of the above affected by his/her illnesses or disabilities?

Is special equipment or extra space, or extra staff time, required in connection with any of the above?

Figure 20c: Page three

Page Four

Summary of care plan proposed, with services and/or proposed placement. List agencies/services to be approached:

Views on proposed services or placement

Client's views:

Views of client's main support person at home:

Views of other key services/people

Signed: Date:

Figure 20d: Page four

college or, in the case of a child, school. Page three constitutes a summary of the features of the client's performance together with statements about the extent to which performance is affected by health, disability or other factors. The page also contains space for comments on staffing or the equipment requirements for any particular activities in the light of health problems or disabilities. The fourth page is set aside for the views of the client and the main support person, as well as the social worker concerning the proposed referral in the context of an overall programme/plan.

It is suggested that this format, with amendments to suit individual agency requirements, could form the basis of an assessment document or profile for a wide range of situations. For example, it could be used in connection with fostering, although in this case a much fuller documentation would be required regarding the child to be fostered. It could be used, for example, in connection with referrals for respite as part of a programme for community care. As already suggested, it could be used as a referral for a day service.

On-going assessments or reviews

An updated network diagram can usefully be incorporated in any on-going assessment or review. It is perhaps easiest to explain the purpose of diary keeping to a client if it is seen to be before or after a particular event. Examples would include:

Before or after moving house.

While unemployed and subsequently after work has been found.

While attending a day service and ceasing to attend that service.

Before entering sheltered accommodation and subsequently.

Network analysis may also be incorporated in the implementation of a specific programme plan. For example, supposing it is part of a programme plan of a person who has left a hospital with mental health problems. Let us say that part of the programme for this person involves getting out more from home. (An example of this kind of situation is to be found in *Case Studies 3 - Towards Independent Living* (Chapter 2).)

Another example of the use of network analysis in connection with the implementation of a care programme would be in work with people with addictions. People suffering from addictions - for example, alcohol related problems or drug abuse - lead lives which are often dominated by the addiction, even when they have stopped taking the drink or drug. Part of a programme might be to help the client diversify his interests, to join in more normal activities and to make friends with people other than fellow addicts or ex-addicts. At the same time the person concerned may need appropriate support from groups or day services where other people who had suffered from similar past addictions meet. Network analysis can monitor the client's progress towards independence from the addiction. In such cases, diaries might be kept at six-monthly intervals. An updated version of the schedules can be used regarding social setting and social background but it would be necessary to go through the full schedule each time both in respect of features of performance and to find the three most significant people, places or activities in the client's life. A suggested format for an updating schedule, which also incorporates the client's views on changes that have taken place, is suggested in Figure 21.

Agencies may have their own procedures and formats and network analysis does not displace these. In the long run, it should be possible to combine elements of existing procedures with the network analysis approach that has been suggested.

Experience to date suggests that network analysis, in field social work, including case management, has the dual purpose of providing, firstly, a basis for assessment or review and, secondly, an experience which can help the client to express his or her views, to formulate his or her problems and, in general, to gain confidence in communication. Experience also suggests that the advantage of this particular approach in any assessment is that the social worker is bound to be confronted by the views of the client through the diaries and, specifically, through the views schedules.

Perhaps clients accept, and often enjoy, keeping diaries for the social worker because it suggests their lives are valued. The client has the opportunity of presenting information in a considered way to the social worker. The social worker, in turn, is forced to read and take notice of what is written. It is appreciated that not all clients express themselves equally readily. For some, the action of keeping a diary will help to improve their capacity to communicate. In other cases, the diary support person can act as a kind of advocate. In other cases, yet again, the diary can be the means of the main support person working with the client in formulating a view of the client's pattern of daily living. Social workers, and field social

Page One

Update and review regarding __________________ (client)

Date:

Date of last assessment/review:

Changes: (Tick if no change)
Address and telephone:

Household composition:

Accommodation and neighbourhood:

Disability/health issues:

Social/behavioural issues:

Has any helpful additional information been obtained regarding the client's past? *(State source of information)*:

Progress or regression regarding: (tick if no change)
Self-management activities:

Daily living activities:

Social activities and interaction:

Has any specific learning taken place since the last review? If so, what?

Figure 21a: Format for update and review schedule (page one)

Page Two *(as for assessment - see Figure 20b)*

Page Three

Review of present services or placement

Client's views:

Record comments and use score where helpful:

1 = Excellent, super
2 = Good
3 = Neither particularly good or bad. Satisfactory.
4 = Not good enough
7 = Deplorable

Views of main support person at home (See above score):

Views of key worker:

Views of other key services:

Summary of progress or regress in the context of overall care plan:

Proposed changes in overall plan and other services to be approached:

Next objectives within this plan:

Signed:

Figure 21b: Pages two and three

workers in particular, have long accepted the importance of taking seriously the client's views in the context of an understanding of the social setting. Network analysis provides the tools for doing this.

Discussion exercises

1. Write down (a) in the form of a narrative and (b) as a diagram, the referral process in the case of a child (or other client) recently referred to you. Afterwards consider if there were benefits in using a diagram.

2. Complete the referral form (Figure 20) or the review form (Figure 21) for a client you have recently been working with.

Chapter 6

Social work in a residential setting

In this chapter we consider the application of network analysis to social work in a variety of residential settings, excluding long-stay hospitals. (Long-stay hospitals will be considered in Chapter 7.)

It is perhaps helpful to consider working with children and young people and working with adults separately. Work with children includes social work in residential schools, children's homes, hostels, halfway houses and communities.

Residential settings for children

Because of shift systems of working and because of the complexity of many residential establishments, no single member of staff will know, from direct experience, the whole day experiences of a child's life. Various devices are used by staff to develop a coherent picture. Log books or incident books, for example, are often kept. Minutes are kept of staff meetings and reports of staff discussions. But how can we put together a picture of what each member of staff means to a particular child? Can we get a picture of what the other children in a residential setting mean to each child? Network analysis provides a means of gaining a clearer picture of what it means to be a child in a residential setting.

The simplest form of diary is required for children to complete and a week is probably sufficient time for the exercise to take place without a break. Figure 15 (page 54) shows the format that was used in a study of children at a residential school. During the week that the child kept the diary, each member of staff kept notes of contacts with the child during the same week. These were put together to give a full picture of both the formal and informal activities in the child's daily life. In the case of formal activities, each staff member concerned stated their particular intentions or objectives for each child. Nine children were studied simultaneously. Each member of staff was asked for details of their contacts during the preceding week regarding any or all of these children. The notes from each staff member were cut and pasted on a separate page for each of the children. (I found it simpler to do this with a stapler and a pair of scissors, but it could of course be done on a word processor.)

Amongst the benefits likely to accrue from this kind of exercise are the following:

1. A child is able to express his or her feelings about people, places and activities within the school and on school excursions or activities elsewhere, including visits home that occurred during the monitored period.
2. Staff are able to assess the role of each member of staff in relation to a particular child during a given week. This will include not only assessing key relationships but also what could be called secondary relationships. By a 'secondary relationship', I mean a relationship a child has with members of staff with whom they are *not* particularly involved. Such relationships - for example with a domestic helper or cook or for that matter a house parent or teacher who is not particularly important in the obvious sense to the child - can nonetheless be important just because they are casual. It is interesting to know what a staff person's feelings are about a child, if this staff person only knows a child to say 'hello' to, or when a child has perhaps the opportunity to perform some courteous gesture.

Relationship qualities are studied, both within the school (or residential home or other residential establishment) and in relation to people, places and activities outside the establishment. For example, within the school, the child is asked to name its three most important activities and the three most important people. It is emphasised that the child is open to make a choice from amongst staff or other children. It will be found that some children are more staff-oriented and others more children-oriented.

It can be expected that there will be a lot of variation in the quality of diary entries. Often, however, it will be found that it is the children of whom least may be known, who have the most to communicate through diaries.

For example, in one case a boy who was shy found the diary a good medium for conveying to members of staff the difficulties he experienced in a group.

Network analysis is helpful in comparing the residential setting with the child's experiences at home. It is necessary, therefore, to ask parents (or other carers) to co-operate during holiday periods, or perhaps during weekend leave. This will help the child and the staff to put the whole of the child's life together. Some children will fantasise about home while they are at school, but what is the reality like? A diary kept at home will help to give us the answers.

Diaries kept by children can have other spin-offs. They can help with literacy. In the case of a residential school, it may be appropriate sometimes for the English teacher to be the diary support person. Children who find difficulties in keeping diaries can also nominate a member of staff or another child to help them. Diaries will most commonly be kept at bedtime and it is useful if it is regarded as a normal activity for children to be writing diaries, quietly, before they go to sleep.

Apart from the diaries, the features of performance schedule will provide a useful framework for reviewing what the child is capable of doing, and not doing, in a broad context related to daily life. Social background and history are already likely to be kept in existing records but it is useful to check that the basic information contained in the social setting and background schedule is known and updated. The views schedule can be completed, with benefit, in interviews with the child and the child's parents or other carers.

An underlying *function* of the exercise as a whole is to compare staff perspectives, children's perspectives and parents' perspectives. There can often be surprises. For example, perhaps a child is good at something at home which he appears not to perform at school - or vice versa. Perhaps the child shows that he or she has an entirely different perspective of what the staff are trying to do. More frequently, however, there may be confirmation, but necessary confirmation, that the aims which the staff are trying to pursue for the child are generally understood and appreciated. The exercise may also reveal or confirm the importance of any particular relationships the child has with other children. In one situation the diaries showed the importance of a relationship between two children, both of whom had suffered sexual abuse. In neither case was this a revelation to the staff, but it was useful to know that the children could gain support from one another.

Diaries and network drawings prepared after an interval of several months may be particularly important. Changes that occur during the child's residential experience can thus be monitored - for example, changes in sleeping arrangements, moves from a main house to a half-way house, or changes in leave arrangements. Network analysis can thus be used for planning within the residential setting and for the child's future; for example, in cases where fostering or adoption are being contemplated. Gains or losses in considering a possible placement can more easily be predicted. Will the child have the opportunity to pursue the activities that he or she is now engaged in? Will he or she have better opportunities than at present?

Residential settings for adults

Residential settings for adults will include hostels and houses for particular client groups, adults living in communities, sheltered or supported housing schemes and homes for the elderly. Some of these situations are discussed in *Case Studies 3 - Towards Independent Living*. In that book we argue that inter-dependent living is in many ways a more appropriate concept than independent living since none of us is realistically totally independent of others. It is also argued that the idea of inter-dependent living is appropriate for the elderly as much as for the adolescent. Network analysis provides a means of assessing and facilitating a more inter-dependent lifestyle through the process of networking. It focuses on the issues which are important in inter-dependent living; namely, relationship qualities, features of performance and patterns and structures of daily life.

Most work with adults in residential settings concerns particular groups of people or people with particular sets of problems - for example, people with drink related problems or drug related problems, ex-offenders, ex-hospital patients or people who are elderly and infirm. With all of these groups it is important to assess the potentiality for developing normal social networks. For example, people with a drugs problem need to learn to move away from a way of life dominated by the drugs scene. Network analysis will help to assess how far this is being been achieved. Ex-offenders and others from institutions may be resident in small houses or in supported or sheltered housing units with a view to developing their capacity to live a normal life in the community. Understanding and developing their social networks is an essential part of this.

In most cases, diaries will be kept for a fortnight. In cases where the residential setting is complex it may be necessary to devise a diary structure which makes it clear where particular activities are taken place. For example, in a residential village community it will be necessary to distinguish between activities pursued in a particular house where the resident lives and elsewhere in the community, as well as activities outside the community altogether.

Residential work with adults is about facilitating and developing opportunities in daily living. The diary is the most effective means of recording existing patterns of daily living and to monitor progress.

Case study

This is a case study of network analysis recently undertaken with a resident whom we will call Charlie, aged 46, and staff in a house, shared by eleven other residents, within a larger residential community. The analysis in this case was conducted by a student on placement. The indented paragraphs are the words of the student herself.

> Charlie suffers from schizophrenia and has a mild mental handicap. This condition distracts him often and prevents him from acting to his full potential. He is a quiet man who appears fairly isolated from the other residents but he is well liked within the hostel. His communication is minimal and others have to start any conversations. His response is usually with one word answers.

This was the first time that network analysis had been used in this residential establishment and the student outlines the reasons for the choice of this particular client:

1. To highlight important people and activities within the client's life.
2. To gain more information about the client's life outside the hostel, i.e. his college and day centre, etc.
3. To encourage communication in general. To help the client to become more talkative on a daily basis about his day, whom he met, what activities he was involved in and those he enjoyed.
4. To encourage the client to use and strengthen his writing ability.

5. To find out whether the client does 'take in' aspects of his day. Does he miss out in the majority of his activities due to his psychotic illness? Is he involved in his life actively?
6. The key worker has an agreement with the client to keep the diary to ensure that appointments with the doctor and clinic etc. are kept. Hopefully the client will become more independent by taking more responsibility in relation to appointments.

The social setting and social background schedule tells us that Charlie was brought up in a house in a large city. He is still in touch with his mother and sister. He attended an ordinary primary school followed by a special school. He then went out to work. He had a job in an ice cream factory, later as a cellar boy in a pub. At the age of about 18, however, he was admitted to a long-stay hospital where he remained for twenty-two years. As part of a rehabilitation plan he spent four years at one house and then transferred to a second house within the same village, i.e. residential community, where he now lives. It is stated on the schedule that Charlie was considered suitable for greater integration within the community outside. He was asked, and agreed, to the move to his present hostel. This was four years ago, after spending four years at the first house after leaving hospital.

The features of performance schedule tells us that Charlie is now good at all self-management skills, including progress that has been made in basic communication. It is stated that he has made progress in expressing *his* views. Some problems arise in daily living skills, for example in cooking - even with a simple snack like beans on toast and a hot drink. He needs assistance to regulate heat and requires a lot of support - or prompting - because he has little motivation. It is stated that he has participated in a cooking skills project and has learnt many aspects of cooking 'as he had never before prepared meals for himself'. In considering more complex cooking, it is stated that Charlie can prepare most meals of his choice, as long as he has the assistance and support he requires. He also now actively participates in preparing supper for himself and other residents. He understands money, can go out and about by himself - including using public transport - and can perform other routine daily living tasks. A comment under the heading 'social learning', however, states that he is often unaware of other people's needs due to his psychotic illness. Sometimes he needs 'encouragement and prompting to trigger any response or awareness', although he is now slightly more aware of other's needs than he used to be.

Charlie attends an adult training centre and the views schedules give an insight into his views about this. The activity he most enjoys is swimming, followed by horse riding and basket or tray making. He comments favourably on a new instructor. Charlie also attends college on some days where he learns reading and writing. The key staff person's views (at the hostel) are also recorded. These views broadly coincide with Charlie's but it is interesting that the staff person gives basket and tray making a far more unfavourable score than Charlie himself does, commenting that it is too repetitive and not stimulating enough. Other activities that the staff person mentions which are important to Charlie include visits to the pub, reading and painting (alone) and attending outside clubs.

A fuller view of Charlie's pattern of living, and his comments about this, are however, contained in diaries which, in this case, were kept for a three-week period. The hostel-based and day centre-based networks are shown respectively in Figures 22-23. The diaries are written by Charlie himself, but with considerable support from whichever member of staff happened to be around at the time. A completed diary page for one of the days is shown in Figure 24.

As will be seen, a typical diary from someone like Charlie, contains the names of many people. When the diaries are complete the key worker will sort out precisely who is who and then ask Charlie in the follow up to name the people, as well as the places and the activities, which are most important out of all the ones he has mentioned. Charlie chose to mention and discuss the manager of the day centre as well as one of the instructors and the organiser at one of the clubs he attends. As a general comment, it was stated that:

> 'Charlie, due to his psychotic illness, appears unaware of other people's needs. But he has a definite awareness of people in charge - with the authority - leadership. This is linked to his past experience in hospital. He recognises the importance and need for people in charge to organise and arrange activities.'

In assessing the value and outcome of the network analysis exercise, the student who co-ordinated it comments:

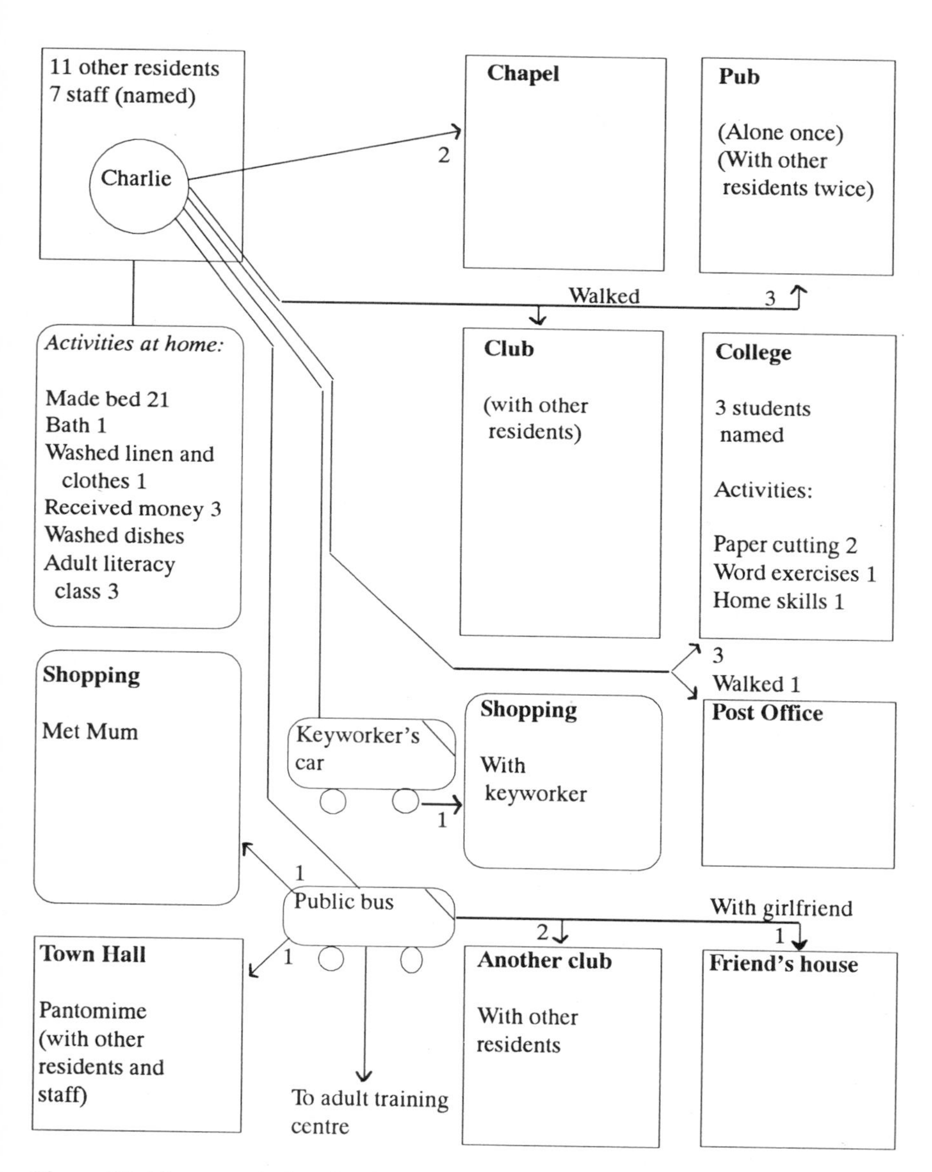

Figure 22: Three weeks in Charlie's life (home-based network)

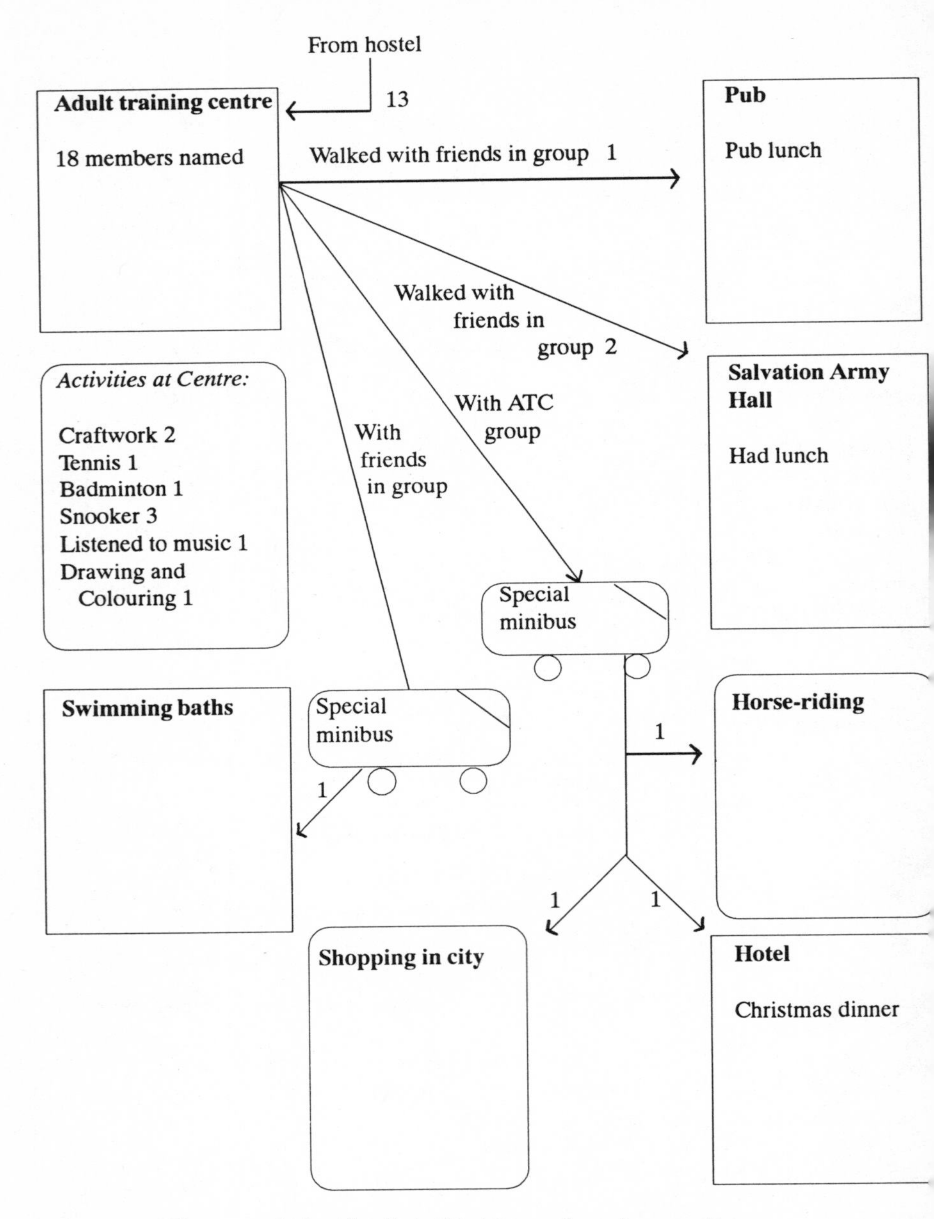

Figure 23: Three weeks in Charlie's life (Centre-based network)

Daily Diary For: CHARLIE For .... (Date) 28.NOV.1988....

	WHAT HAPPENED? WHAT DID YOU DO?	WHO WERE YOU WITH?	WHO DID YOU MEET?
MORNING	SHAVE WASH BREAKFAST COMB MY HAIR MADE MY BED WENT TO THE CENTRE PLAY AT TENNIS	WITH WENT TO THE CENTENARY DOUGLAS LEON BILLY ALAN JOSEPH BRIAN RALPH	EILEEN IRENE PATRICIA OFFICER IN CHARGE SECRETARY GIRLFRIEND
LUNCH-TIME	WENT TO THE SALVATION ARMY HALL AND HAD LUNCH	BILLY BRIAN LEON	
AFTERNOON	GYM PLAYED BADMINTON WENT TO THE DINNER HALL TEA AND BISCUIT WENT TO THE CLASSROOM	LEON JOSEPH	MET DOUGLAS'S FRIENDS
EVENING (NIGHT)	ATTENDED THE C.L. CLASS AT HOME	DAVID MY TUTOR AND THREE RESIDENTS WILLIE JESS AND MARY	THE OTHER TUTORS MOIRA GRACE AND JEAN

WHAT JOURNEYS DID YOU MAKE FROM HOME?

TO:	HOW DID YOU TRAVEL?	WHO WERE YOU WITH?	WHO DID YOU MEET?
B---- [illegible] CENTRE	BUS	MAN	GEORGE BUS DRIVER

Add comments on the back of this sheet if you wish: e.g. if the day was very unusual. If anyone helped you complete the diary, their comments are also welcome.

Figure 24: A page of Charlie's completed diary.

'Staff are now are very aware of how much the client *is involved* in his daily activities. They are aware of the activities he prefers and gets most enjoyment from. Discussing the diary has highlighted important relationships i.e. key worker, friends in the local pub etc. Overall, the analysis has shown that the centre is very much part of his life and he is happy with his networks at present.

Communication-wise, the client is slowly initiating conversation on his own with encouragement. He is now seeing the need and importance of speaking with others and sharing his daily activities.

It has been a slow process encouraging the client to communicate but over several months there is a definite improvement. It is important to note that owing to the long time spent in hospital, communication is something the client views as not necessary - the hospital setting being one of large thirty-bedded wards and few staff, with physical care at most being dealt with by staff.

From three weeks' diary writing the client is now keeping his own diary from choice. This seems to be encouraging him to talk more of his day as he is writing it down when he has free time. This is also helping him with his appointments as arranged by the client and key worker. The key worker is very pleased with the client's initiative.

From the analysis, more information was found out in relation to the client's past employment. Nobody had known about his paid employment - there were no records of it in the files.

More information was also collected in relation to his schooling. This is something which has made staff perhaps more keen in finding out more about other residents' employment and schooling as, for all residents, their files have minimal information.

It is interesting to find that even within the final discussion with the client, the key worker and myself, the client was giving us more information that he had noticed was missing from the diagrams, activities which he had missed out when keeping his diary! This was seen as a very positive. The client was initiating conversation and information about himself.'

This case was presented to a seminar organised by the Central Council for Education and Training and Social Work.

Discussion exercises

1. Which children would you first select in your residential setting for keeping a network analysis? What are the reasons for your choice?

2. Discuss the case of Charlie, on the basis of the information given in the text and in Figures 22-24. How has the network analysis exercise helped Charlie and in what ways will the exercise assist staff in future planning with him?

Chapter 7

People leaving long-stay and other hospitals

Network analysis has been used as a means of studying residents in long-stay hospital both prior to discharge and when they have subsequently moved into the community. It provides a means of assessing their quality of life both within a hospital and in the community.

A diary form is used which distinguishes between activities within the hospital ward, activities outside the ward but within the hospital and activities outside the hospital. Where the social worker already has a particularly close relationship with the patient it may be sensible for him or her to make the necessary arrangements directly with the patient. It other circumstances, however, the diary support person is likely to be the nurse in charge of the ward. Where possible, patients should be encouraged to keep their own diaries with appropriate support, but it is sometimes difficult to avoid a situation where it is assumed that nursing staff will keep diaries for patients. Where patients cannot write their own diaries, it is essential that nursing staff allow the patients to participate, and that as far as possible, they dictate the contents of the diary entries. The diary form used in hospital is shown in Figure 14 (page 51).

Features of performance schedules will be completed with the patient usually in company with the nurse on duty. The completion of the schedules causes some problems because of the frequent lack of opportunity in a hospital setting for patients to attempt any daily living skills on their own. For example, how do we know whether a patient can prepare baked beans on toast and a pot of tea? He or she is not likely to have the opportunity to do this on the ward. It is possible that such an activity will form part of a programme of training but this is likely to be in another part of the hospital

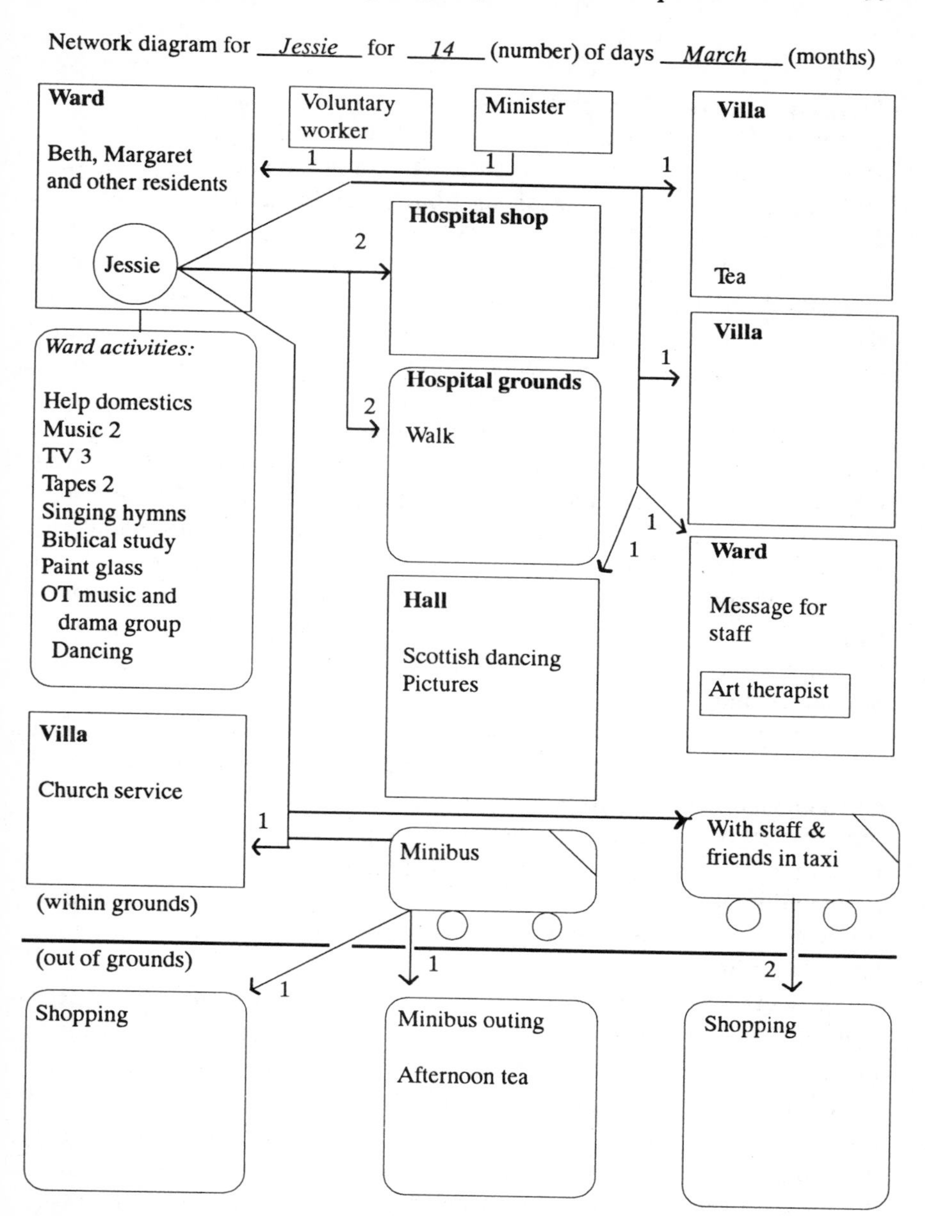

Figure 25: 14 days in Jessie's life in hospital

and the ward staff will not necessarily know much about it. One can, and does, ask the patient himself or herself but, to obtain a staff perspective on the degree of support or assistance required, it is necessary to see therapists or whoever is responsible, and even then the situation in which daily living skills are practised is often artificial. I have found that the best clues as to the patient's potential is often found by asking about holidays. Many patients have holidays which may involve a more normal living situation in which daily living skills are exercised. Indeed, nursing staff who have accompanied patients on holidays have often been surprised at the abilities that patients have shown, particularly if the holiday involved self-catering.

Although the exercise of obtaining the information necessary for network analysis is sometimes time consuming, the result is rewarding in a hospital setting. Patients, sometimes even within the same ward, can lead very different lifestyles in hospital. Many people left in long-stay hospitals today are elderly. It is possible to make false assumptions about the restricted lives such patients lead. Figure 25 shows the network for a fortnight in the case of an elderly lady with a mental handicap in a long-stay hospital. As a result of this exercise it was concluded that a move to the community would be too traumatic and unsettling and would not necessarily enrich her social life.

Network analysis in a long stay hospital can be of crucial importance in locating friendship patterns and their significance. It has revealed in some cases that patients can suffer when close friends are separated from them in the process of a piece-meal discharge of patients from hospital to the community. In many cases it would be beneficial if patients moved into the community with their friends. In some hospitals, group patient plans allow this to happen. Network analysis provides the evidence on which to proceed along these lines.

Network analysis is consistent with a client-needs-led approach instead of a facility-led approach. The differences between these two approaches is presented in diagrammatic form in Figure 26. This has a wider application than people leaving long-stay hospitals. The problems in implementing a client needs approach are particularly difficult to recognise with the planning complexities involved in a discharge of people from long-stay institutions. I was recently involved in the undertaking of this task with a voluntary organisation with the collaboration of the hospital concerned. Patients to be discharged were duly identified after careful study involving network

a) The person-oriented approach

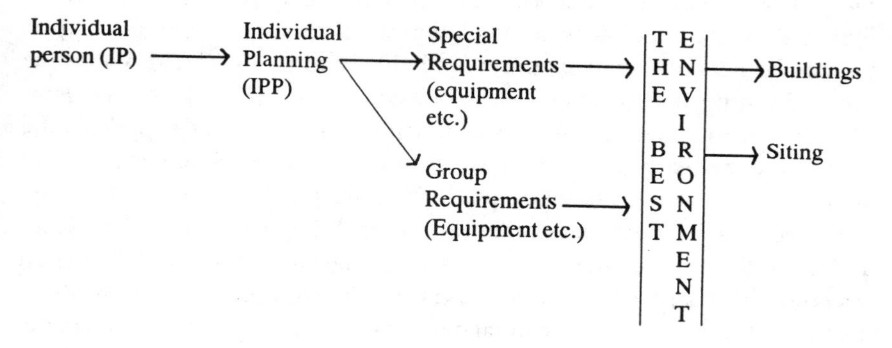

b) The facility-oriented approach

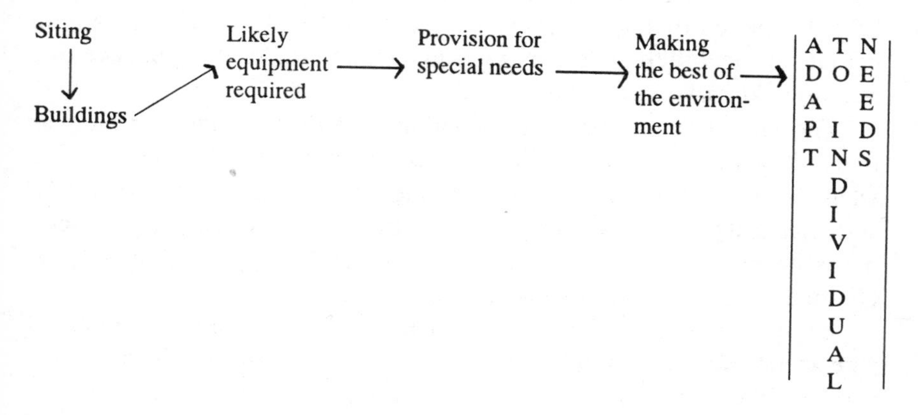

Figure 26: Two approaches to planning

analysis, but the action response in terms of providing the community facilities that were required as a result of the exercise proved to be slow and difficult. The selection of the patients had involved discussions with parents or other carers of patients who felt they had the right to veto plans - even in the case of patients who had been in hospital for many years and with whom they had little contact. It is my view that while the patient's main support person for network analysis purposes is likely to be identified within the hospital setting, account should also be taken at an early stage of the views of people who regard themselves as having been sources of support in the past. They are likely to be involved, if they live in the same geographical area, after the move has taken place from hospital into the community. Advocacy for the client takes the form of enabling the client to speak out and assert their independence in the face of what can sometimes be parental uncertainty or anguish. In other cases the opposite may occur. A client discharged from long-stay hospital may wish to renew contact with parents who are reluctant to want to know anything about the client. In either case, network analysis provides a framework for incorporating the views of all concerned and, using key members in the network who have been identified, helps facilitate a dialogue. For example, in some cases it may be fruitful for parents to meet with clients in a group situation under the guidance of a social worker who has group work skills.

The data from network analysis will provide the basis on which to plan in detail, with the client, for life in the community. It enables us to assess what degree of support or assistance the client needs for the particular activities that he wishes to pursue. It will also clarify what degree of support or assistance is required in self management, e.g. dressing, feeding, bathing, climbing stairs and communicating with others.

Experience suggests that network analysis helps us to see community care in pro-active, dynamic terms. It is not a case of simply providing accommodation with an appropriate level of staffing or domicilliary support. Building on what the client was able to do in hospital, one can develop a programme with goals for life in the community. For example, many people, when hospital patients, have the opportunity to undertake domestic work. If a particular patient likes doing this, can this lead into a work programme leading to employment in the community? Not all such patients may want this, of course.

Network analysis will also provide a means of assessing the quality of life and progress that the client has made at measured intervals after leaving hospital. Examples of this are provided in the first chapter of *Case Studies for Practice 1* which studied the progress of two people several years after they had left a long-stay hospital.

Network analysis provides a means of evaluating different approaches to community care. The examples in *Case Studies for Practice 1* are what could be called a step-by-step approach. The patients concerned left hospital initially to go to a village community. Within that community they graduated through a hostel with maximum support to a house with less support and eventually to a shared tenancy in a cottage just outside the hospital grounds. They moved from there to an ordinary tenancy in the community. This approach has been criticised on the grounds that people do not normally move houses in accordance with their levels of progression towards independent living. Instead, it has been suggested that the level of support should change and initially, perhaps, that staff should move out from hospital to live with the patients in the community. There are other approaches, including core and cluster arrangements and supported landlady schemes.

Wherever they are placed, patients who have left long-stay hospital are likely to need continuous help and support not only in living 'independently' but in living, in a social sense, more *inter-dependently*. This involves networking techniques which were discussed in Chapter 2. Networking must be based on the sound understanding of existing, as well as, potential social networks.

Network analysis can be helpful in preparing for discharge from short-term as well as long-term hospital care. This applies in any situation where attendance as an in-patient is going to affect the home situation or where the client's illness will have implications for changes in life-style after discharge.

Discussion exercises

1. Consider the possible benefits of a network analysis approach in selecting a small group of patients to move out together from hospital to community care. What criteria for selection of patients, and what options for different forms of housing and support, would be more important?

2. What features of Jessie's network (Figure 25) give cause for reflection before any decision were to be made to discharge her to the community.

3. Consider in detail the uses of network analysis in relation to short-term hospital care and subsequently.

4. Discuss Figure 26.

Chapter 8

Day services

Day services are provided to a wide range of clients - in fact virtually every client group one can think of, from children and families to people who are elderly and disabled, as well as to specific groups such as those suffering from alcohol related or drug addiction problems. Day services, understood in a positive and purposeful context, occupy a pivotal position in a total programme of education and training, care and rehabilitation. On the one hand, social workers and others working in day services have continuous periods of contact with clients and, therefore, are in a position to know them thoroughly. On the other hand, social learning activities through day services are meaningless unless the learning is transferred to home and community settings. Day service staff are well placed to develop contacts with the client's main support people at home on a regular basis. In these ways, they can be regarded as pivotal, relating both to the client's home background and to the network of services available in and through the community. This proposition is illustrated in Figure 27.

The ways in which diaries are kept reflect these possibilities. It is suggested that two separate diaries are kept, one at home and one at the centre. Figure 28 shows a suitable diary to be kept at home on a day where a client attends at the centre. Figure 29 suggests the format for a diary kept with staff help at the centre itself. An additional schedule (Figure 30) has been successfully used to elicit statements of aims on the part of staff for each activity with the client. The findings from the two sets of diaries and the schedule can be usefully compared to see precisely how activities at the centre fit in with activities the client pursues at home.

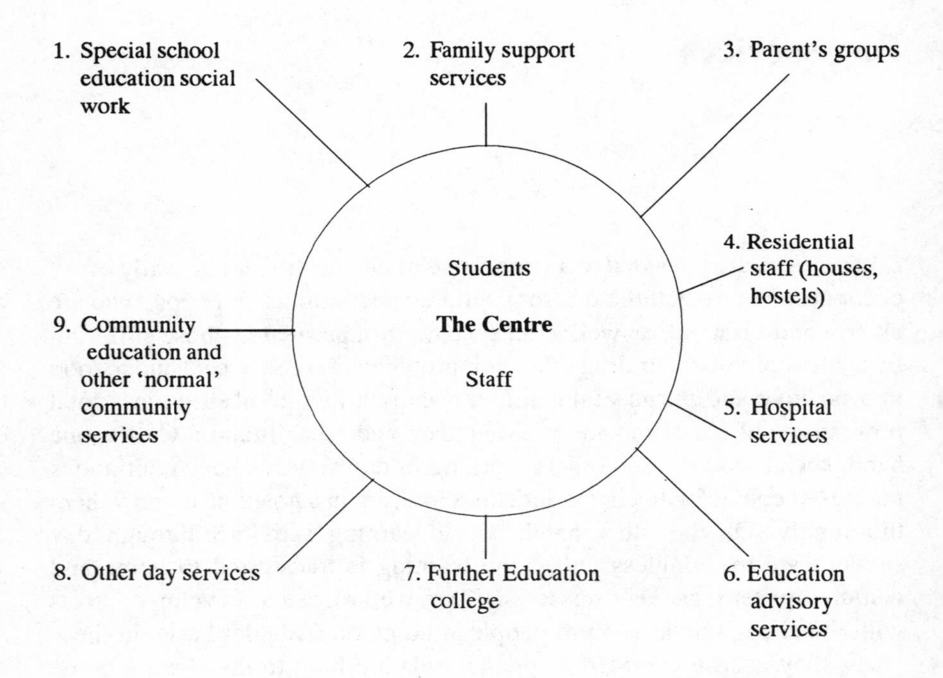

Figure 27: The position of a model day service in relation to home support and local services

Diary kept at home for days spent at centre

Name ______________ For ______________ Day date ______________

	List events or activities you can remember while you were at home (or hostel etc.)	Who were you with? If lots of people, name important people (If necessary, explain who they are)
What happened today: 1. Before going to the Centre		
2. During the day at the Centre		
3. During the evening or night		

4. Did you go out anywhere after returning from the centre?

Places visited	Who with?	How did you travel?	Event or activity	Who else did you meet?

Additional comments from person who assisted in completing diary

Figure 28: Diary format for a day at the Centre (kept by client at home)

Diary kept at centre for

_______ day _______ date _______ name

	What events or activities can you remember?	Who were you with? If lots of people, name important people (If necessary, explain who they are)
What happened today: 1. On the way to the centre		
2. During the morning		
3. Lunch-time		
4. During the afternoon		

5. Did you go out anywhere after returning from the centre?

Places visited	Who with?	How did you travel?	Event or activity	Who else did you meet?

6. Did anything happen today that you want to comment on further?

7. Additional comments from person who assisted in completing diary (*Continue over page if necessary*)

Figure 29: Format for client diary kept at day centre

Record and coding for staff statements
relating to activities, objectives and problems

Client
Staff

Activity and code	Importance code	Statements about objectives and code*	Problems mentioned and code
Activity status: ☐		*First objective:* ☐☐☐☐	*First problem:* ☐☐
		Second objective: ☐☐☐☐	*Second problem:* ☐☐
		Third objective: ☐☐☐☐	*Third problem:* ☐☐

Key to activity status code

In terms of time spent, was this
a main activity........................1
a major activity......................2
a minor activity......................3
an activity which was
incidental to some
other activity........................4

Key to importance code:

In terms of importance, was this
Crucially important..................1
Important..................................2
Quite important........................3
Not particularly important.......4
Not important...........................5
Other answers...........................9

Key to problems code:

Behavioural.......................1
Learning difficulty............2
Not enough time...............3
Lack of equipment...........4
Lack of space....................5
Lacks concentration.........6
Other.................................9

* For an example of coding for objectives see Seed, P., (1988), *Day Care at the Crossroads*, Costello

Figure 30: Format for interview with key staff person regarding objectives for each activity with client

In our extensive studies of day services in Scotland, we have found various anomalies that network analysis has revealed. Some of the most obvious are the following:

A client travels independently by public bus from home but is dependent on special centre-based transport to get to and from the centre.

A client has a very restrictive life at home with very few visits out. This is compensated for by an extensive network of activities from the centre into the community.

The opposite of this - that is to say, the client has an extensive network of contacts at home but has a restricted pattern of activities at the centre.

The client performs daily living tasks at home, which they are not allowed to do or not able to do at the centre (and vice versa).

The client demonstrates an ability to engage in work activities at home which are not available to him or her at the centre.

The client has a quite different pattern of activities at weekends from the pattern of life known to centre staff on week days. (In one case, the client went away from a city with his father to a country cottage and led a quite different life there.)

In other cases, network analysis will reveal the extent to which the institutional routines of the centre dominate life at home. This is again most obvious where special transport not only takes a client to and from a centre but from home to other activities arranged by voluntary clubs - for example, trips to the swimming pool or to weekly clubs. How, it may be asked, in this case, is the client going to learn to use public transport?

Who initiates the network analysis exercise is of secondary importance. In one interesting situation the initiative was taken by the staff of a respite care home. This had some advantage in that the staff were slightly detached, both from the client's own home and from the day service. The respite care staff managed to enlist the support of the day services involved and they also visited the client's home. This helped to make respite care more meaningful and it also helped to throw light on the relevance of the day services. Figures 31-32 show the home-based and centre-based networks for one of the clients who attended the respite care home, whom we will call George. The features of performance schedule shows that he is severely handicapped. He can use the toilet 'at times'. He is mostly confined to a

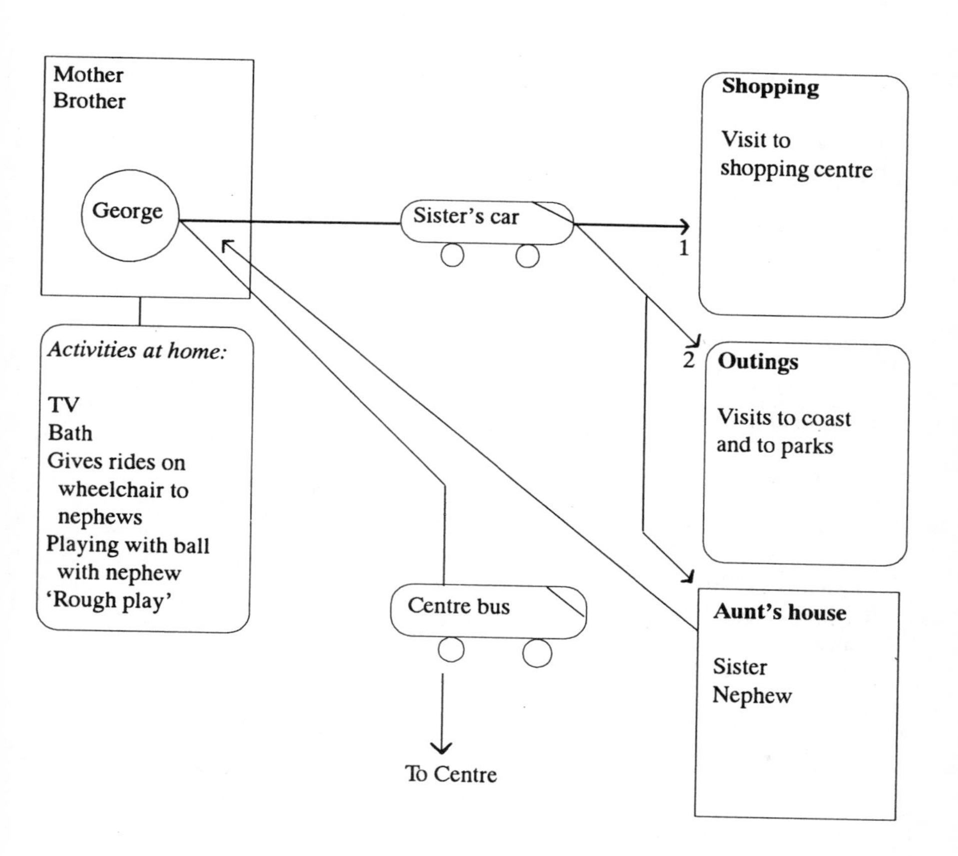

Figure 31: George's home-based network, compiled from respite home

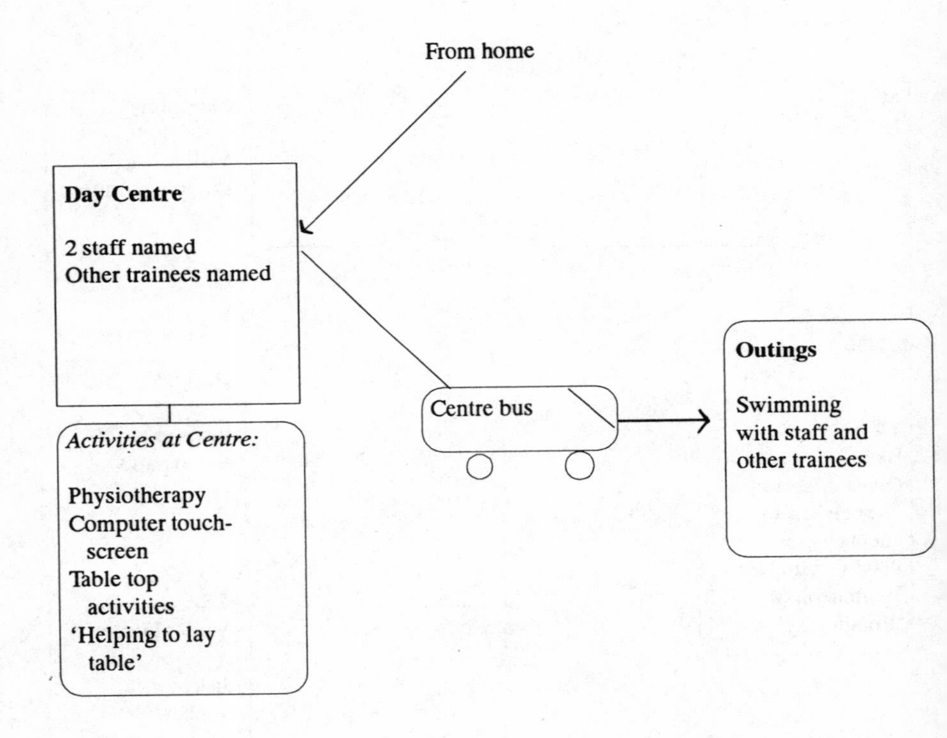

Figure 32: George's Centre-based network, compiled from respite home

wheelchair, although two people together can hold him up to try to walk 'with much support'. He has no spoken communication which could be understood by strangers, but he can manage to communicate choices in food and clothing and make his basic needs known. Although he cannot tell the time, he has an understanding of the time, specifically when he knows the centre bus is overdue.

The analysis in this case revealed that the mother stopped George's attendance at clubs on account of her own ill-health. George is aged twenty-five. What, it may be asked, should a young man of this age be doing in accordance with the principles of normalisation? The centre is, perhaps, rightly concentrating on developing basic abilities through physiotherapy, a computer touch screen, table top activities and exercises in wheelchair use. He is also involved in the centre in such adult activities as helping to lay the tables: 'he likes to help as far as he can, e.g. taking items from kitchen to table etc. He enjoys participation'. George has many physical problems as well as learning difficulties. He is epileptic and quadriplegic. Yet, as well as the swimming, shown in the network, he is also, through the centre, involved in horse riding.

The network analysis identifies the people and the places most significant in George's present life. The day centre is by far the most important place for him and the three named important people were his key worker, another worker at the centre defined as a 'day care/home support worker', and the bus driver who takes him to and from the centre. Of the bus driver, George was able to say that he liked him because 'he makes me laugh'. He added 'he takes me wherever I go in the centre bus'. For someone confined to a wheelchair, this degree of attachment to someone who transports him is understandable.

In another case, whom we will call Susan, network analysis was undertaken by the centre manager. The manager felt it is was an opportunity to get to know her and to have more experience herself of individual clients. Another reason was that there was a possibility that Susan might be considered as one of the clients to move from home, where she currently lives with her mother, to a supported housing scheme run by a voluntary organisation. Apart from the manager's interest, the key worker in this case found out a great deal about Susan, and Susan herself found it helpful by looking at the diagrams to see what she actually did.

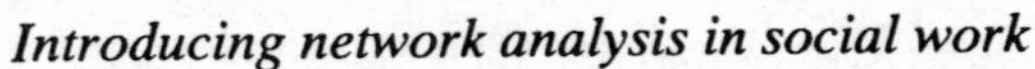

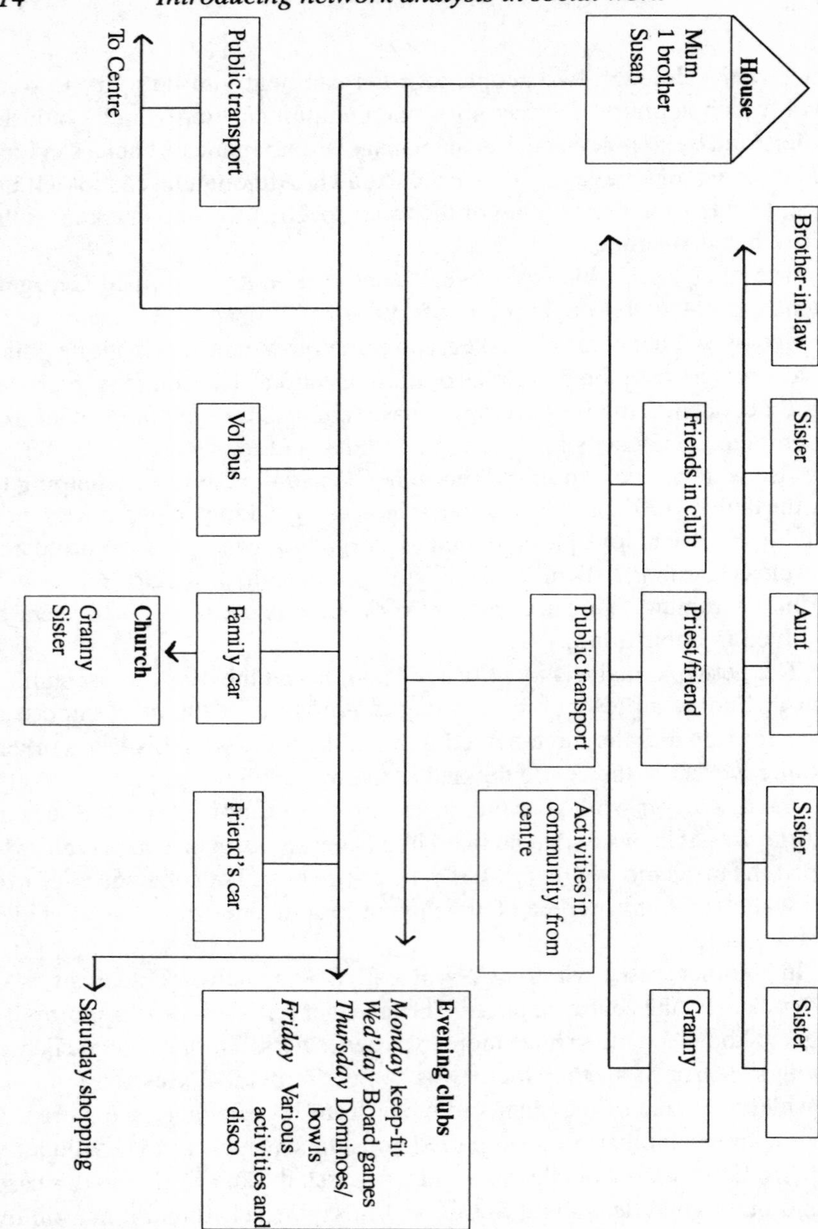

Figure 33: Susan's home network

Activities at Centre Susan is involved in

Domestic training room

Shopping/Cafes

Computer

Further education

Training/flat

Video camera

Education camera slides

Hygiene programme

Shower

Carpet bowls

Hobby - sewing

Core Curriculum

Use of public, community and social facilities with necessary acquisition of a 'social sight' vocabulary;

A working knowledge of shopping transactions;

An ability to deal with public agencies;

The use of public eating places;

The use of public transport;

An awareness of civic responsibilities and rights;

An understanding of normal social conventions and appropriate behaviours;

A general preparation for 'independent living' including 'survival' cookery and personal care

Figure 34: Susan's Centre programme

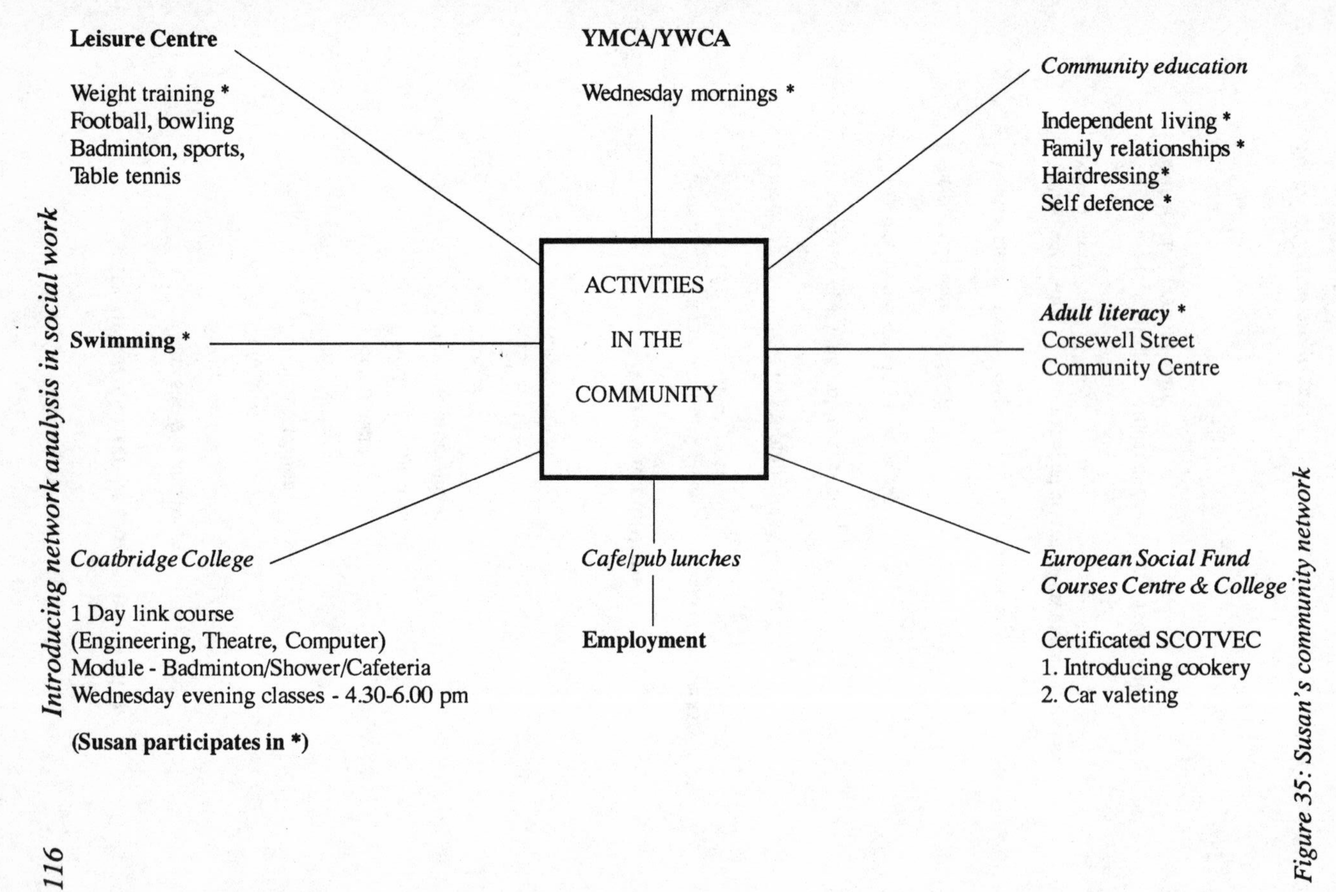

Figure 35: Susan's community network

In this case, the manager adapted the standard network analysis procedures, and these are quoted in full in Figures 33-35. They show the possibility for the practitioner to modify aspects of the detail of network analysis representations in order to scrutinize more carefully particularly aspects of practice. In this instance, they provide a basis for examining the relationship between the core curriculum and other activities at the centre and the client's progress towards greater community involvement.

In another case, at another centre, network analysis was used to study a lady with a profound handicap in her mid-twenties who spent 'all her time in a wheelchair'. She was chosen from an initial network analysis exercise because there was a possibility of her moving to a special care unit. The centre staff were also concerned about the fact that her parents did not come very often to see what was going on. The result of undertaking the exercise was that differences emerged between what the staff thought they were providing and what the client was in fact experiencing. It was discovered that the parents had in the past had repeated bad experiences at earlier day centres which influenced their attitudes towards the present centre. The centre staff also discovered, for the first time, why it was that the parents insisted on bringing the client by car to the centre, even though she lived only a few hundred yards away. This was to do with the physical difficulty of moving the client and the parents' inability to undertake this single-handed.

Examples of a wide range of other client's situations in connection with the use of day centres, based on network analysis, are to be found in the *Case Studies for Practice* series and in other publications.[1] It is the area of social work practice where there has been most experience in network analysis to date.

Reference

1. Seed, P., (1988), *Day Care at the Crossroads.* Costello.

Discussion exercises

1. Discuss the two approaches to planning (Figure 26) with reference to your own agency or provision.

2. Fill in the details for your own centre under the headings suggested in Figure 27.

3. Practice filling in the form shown in Figure 30. Has this exercise made you think more precisely about your work with individual clients?

4. How far do the visual representations in Figures 33-35 provide a useful basis for assessing the centre's core curriculum and other activities as a basis for promoting Susan's quality of life at home and in the community?

Chapter 9

Management, planning and the monitoring of services

So far, we have looked at network analysis very much from the point of view of the social work practitioner. It is important to remember, however, that the techniques began, as research techniques, dealing not just with single client networks but with large samples. For example, the networks of several hundred clients were studied in the Scottish Highlands and Islands in 1978, and one-hundred and forty-six client networks were studied, in a more recent evaluation, of day services in Scotland.[1,2]

In research and monitoring of services, as in research, the focus changes from individual networks to a comparison between features of many different networks. For example, we might want to know how many clients live in particular kinds of neighbourhoods, in particular kinds of households, with particular types of transport and so on. All of this is possible by picking features off individual networks and aggregating their incidence. The network schedules which we use, are ready adapted to this purpose. Boxes by each question allow for computer coding. For example, one application could be to aggregate the incidence of particular features recorded on the referral forms we have suggested.

It has to be said, however, that, to date, we have no experience of these procedures being used for management, as distinct from research, purposes. Obviously, there is no point in such an exercise until the use of network analysis is sufficiently general amongst practitioners. This, indeed, is a problem which we have encountered in training seminars when practitioners, beginning to use network analysis procedures, have found that there are some difficulties unless social workers around them are also adopting the same methods. It would ,therefore, be appropriate to introduce network analysis, as a pilot scheme, in a particular area or team and at that point to use it for management as well as practitioner purposes. Further details of appropriate techniques for this are to be found in another volume.[3]

We have more experience in using network analysis in connection with the planning of services. Reference has already been made to this in relation to the discharge of patients from long-stay hospitals (see Chapter 7).Recent planning exercises have led us to develop a standard procedure for considering the implications of network analysis for groups of people as distinct from a number of individuals, consistent with a client-needs-led approach. The key aspect of this new procedure is the concept of 'growth points'.

After completing each individual's social networks, features of performance and the views of the main support person, a table is completed for each individual client under the following headings:

- name/code
- summary
- growth points

for each growth point:

- general implications
- implications for staffing
- implications for equipment
- implications for environment (e.g. setting and space requirements)
- implications for transport
- implications for the needs of the main support people at home

Growth points are classified according to areas of development using the following code and headings:

10 physical development

20 mobility

30 communication

40 social development

50 sensory:

51 sight

52 hearing

53 touch

54 smell

These headings are relevant to the study of services for people with disabilities. Different headings would be appropriate for other client groups.

Growth points as classified above or using a different system for other client groups are numbered as above for purposes of computerisation. A decimal point is used to prepare data for representation in tabular form for each of the headings indicated earlier. For example 10.11 indicates the first growth point in the area of physical development. 10.21 indicates general implications of this growth point. 10.31 indicates staffing implications. 10.41 indicates equipment implications. 10.51 indicates environment implications. 10.61 indicates transport implications (if any) and 10.71 indicates any implications for the needs of carers.

The following is an example.

Code (identification, age and sex): AR/27/F

Summary: very small and slight. Badly twisted spine. Uses only right arm and hand. Middle child. Close family network. Mother sees potential which is not being developed.

10 physical development:

10.11 weight bearing and walking.

10.21 assess attempts made in past and develop.

10.31 physiotherapist.

10.41 standing frame,walking frame.

10.51 level ground.

10.61 moulded chair in ordinary car. Client sits on seat. Easy to lift.

10.71 work with mother.

Data can thus be stored on computer and, if necessary, reproduced in tabular form with the different areas for growth points along one axis and the various implications on the other axis.

This approach enables the resource implications for each area of development to be listed and aggregated. For example, in a study of thirteen young adults with profound mental and physical handicaps the following data list represented an aggregation of requirements.

Staffing skills required

- exercise skills
- tactile skills
- massage skills
- yoga skills
- sex education
- language development
- behaviour modification
- makaton
- toilet signalling
- computer skills
- music and movement/dance skills
- aroma skills
- gardening enthusiast
- swimming instructor
- hairdressing
- carrying/handling skills
- food preparation

- development worker: link with parents
- counselling skills
- groupwork skills
- volunteers: painting, escort, music, garden, clubs
- respite/residential skills

Additional consultancy skills: physiotherapist, OT, psychologist, speech therapy, consultant on visual handicap especially use of light and shadow, dental care, riding instructor.

Equipment needs

- standing frame
- walking frame
- walking bars
- sitting frame
- cushion supports
- floor cushions
- personal seats
- mobile hoist
- trays for fixing to wheelchairs
- dining tables for wheelchairs
- non-spill cups
- oval plates with deep end spoons
- forks and knives with big handles
- kitchen equipment (for learning use)

- hoover (for learning use)
- music equipment: hi-fi, tape recorders, musical instruments
- (percussion, recorders), earphones, ear muffles
- video camera, TV
- computer suitable for language and communication development
- objects for touching
- paper, paints
- special lighting
- light play equipment
- mobiles
- puzzles
- sense stimuli
- dressing up clothes
- mirrors
- plants
- books
- communication boards
- massage couch
- massage oils
- changing bench for swimming pool
- armbands, floats
- swing
- fish tank

- provision for small animals

Environmental needs

- quiet rooms
- soft play area
- specially warm room
- messy play area
- group play area
- music/dance room
- darkenable room
- room with basin, mirror, hair dryer
- a room for social occasions
- parents' resource/meeting room.
- level ground required from street onwards.
- door handles, switches reachable from wheelchairs, wide door.
- toilet easy to access
- toilets for wheelchair and helper
- bathroom with mobile hoist
- accessible kitchen, dining arrangements for small groups and individuals
- garden, conservatory, garden flowerbeds at wheelchair level, fishpond
- at wheelchair level, animal areas
- hydrotherapy pool
- respite/residential care unit

- sunny areas
- space for large objects (sculptures)
- stage area

Transport needs

- mini-bus with hoist and space for largest wheelchair
- individual seats for private cars

The above, of course, represents an ideal view of what is required. Priorities can then be assessed, dependent on the resources available, but at least we have a list of what is ideally required consistent with a client-needs-led approach. In the example given, substantial funds were available and most of what was set down is expected to be provided.

The next stage was to summarise the above lists in a form suitable for an architect's brief and for costing purposes to the funding bodies.

A similar approach has been used for other studies of the needs of a wider range of people with learning difficulties in specific localities.

Network analysis offers the basis for all-through planning from individual assessment to resource allocation, staffing and building development.

Even with all this attention being given to individual needs, effective planning still depends on coordination between all those concerned. Network analysis provides the methods of ensuring quality control provided such coordination exists.

References

1. Seed, P. *Mental Handicap: Who Helps in Rural and Remote Communities?* Costello, 1980.

2. Seed, P. *Day Care at the Crossroads*. Costello, 1988.

3. Seed, P. *Applied Social Network Analysis*. Costello, 1987.

Appendix

Social network analysis

PRACTITIONER VERSION*

Name of client ....Sex ....Age or DOB ....
Address ....Tel ....
Name of social worker ....Team ....

Social setting

S1V21 Description of accommodation

S1V22 Who else, if anyone, shares the accommodation with the client?

NAME *(if any)*	RELATIONSHIP TO CLIENT *(if any)*
....	....
....	....
....	....

* *A Research version of this schedule is also available*

S1V34 **Name other relatives or close friends *currently* in contact with client (and not living with client)**

NAME (*if any*)	RELATIONSHIP TO CLIENT
....	....
....	....
....	....

S1V43 **Description of neighbourhood**

S1V44 **Client's access to use of car or other private transport (Describe situation)**

S1V46 **Access to key community facilities. Describe accessibility by private or public transport for the client from home (e.g. to post office, essential shopping, GP, sports and leisure facilities, etc.)**

S1V52 **Describe domiciliary support to the client in his/her accommodation**

SUPPORT PERSON(S)	FREQUENCY OF VISITS
....	....
....	....
....	....

Indicate if any one of the above is designated key worker

S1V64 **Describe team support schemes (if any) which operate for this client.**

Social history

S2V21ff **Outline client's history of previous accommodation**

FROM	TO
....	....

....
....

S2V28 Outline client's history of schooling (indicating types of schools attended)

S2V32 Outline client's history since leaving school (include work, training, FE courses, etc.)

Health

S2V44 Does the client have any health problems? If so, give details of past health problems and state if these problems are still active. Add comments on social implications.

PROBLEM *(Tick if active)*	SOCIAL IMPLICATIONS
....	....
....	....
....	....

Disabilities

S2V46 Does the client have sensory impairments or disabilities not referred to under 'health problems' (previous page)?

PROBLEM	SOCIAL IMPLICATIONS
....	....
....	....
....	....

S2V47 Does the client have social or behavioural problems? Tick if these problems are acknowledged by the client as current issues. What are the implications for the client or for others in daily living?

PROBLEM	SOCIAL IMPLICATIONS
....	....
....	....
....	....

Details of main support person (e.g. parent, relative)

Name .... Age ....

Address ....

....

History since leaving school (e.g. work, training, FE etc.)

Details of others who were of key importance to the client in the past

NAME	IMPORTANCE
....	....
....	....
....	....

VIEWS OF (A) CLIENT (B) MAIN SUPPORT PERSON (C) KEY STAFF PERSON

Schedule four (S4) - Client's views

S4V21 Accommodation

What do you think about the house/flat/hostel (or whatever form of accommodation applies) where you live?

Code using graded opinions as follows:

Excellent 1
Good 2
Satisfactory 3
Not good 4
Deplorable 5

In particular:

S4V21	the space available	....
S4V22	comfort	....
S4V23	company (the people you share with)	....
S4V24	where it is - convenience	....
S4V25	staff (where applicable)	....
S4V26	other features (indicate)	....

S4V27ff Place of work or other daytime activity(ies)

What do you think about .... (the place) you attend? In particular:

	the things you do there (specify):	
S4V27	first activity	....
S4V28	second activity	....
S4V29	third activity	....
S4V31	fourth activity	....

Code graded opinions on 1-5 scale

S4V32	the other people you meet there:	....
S4V33	staff there	....
S4V34	transport (how you get there)	....
S4V35	other things about it (specify)	....

S4V36 **Have you ever thought you would like to do something else/go somewhere else other than .... (where you are now)?**

Code as follows:

would like to do something else 1
no, would like to stay where I am 2
other answers 9
don't know ....X ....

S4V37 (*If you would like to do something else*) **What would you prefer you did instead?**

Code as follows:

paid work 1
work training scheme 2
voluntary work 3
FE college 4
stay at home 5
attend a day centre 6
combination of the above (state) 7
other 9
don't know ....X ....

S4V38 **Can you tell me something about your interests of hobbies - the things you like doing - and who you do them with?**

Activity	*Place*	*Who with*
....	....	....
....	....	....
....	....	....

S4V39 **Are there other things you would like to do but do not get the chance to do?**

Activity	*Reason for not doing it*
....	....
....	....
....	....

S4V40 **Client views of domiciliary support services (specify service)**

S4V41 **Other comments on social work or other services in general**

Schedule six (S6) - Main support person's views

S6V21 Accommodation

What do you think about the house/flat/hostel (or whatever form of accommodation applies) where the client lives?

Code using graded opinions as follows:

Excellent 1
Good..2
Satisfactory 3
Not good 4
Deplorable 5

In particular

S6V21	the space available	....
S6V22	comfort	....
S6V23	company (the people the client shares with)	....
S6V24	where it is - convenience	....
S6V25	staff (where applicable)	....
S6V26	other features (indicate)	....

S6V27ff Place of work or other daytime activity(ies)

What do you think about .... (the place) the client attends? In particular:

the things the client does there (specify)

S6V27	first activity	....
S6V28	second activity	....
S6V29	third activity	....
S6V31	fourth activity	....

Code graded opinions on 1-5 scale

S6V32	the other people the client meets there	....
S6V33	staff there	....
S6V34	transport (How the client gets there)	....
S6V35	other things about it (specify)	....
S6V36	have you ever thought the client would like to do something else/ go somewhere else other than .... (where he/she is now)	....

Code as follows:

the client would like to do something else 1
no, the client would like to stay where he/she is 2
other answers 9
don't know ....X ....

S6V37 (*If the client would like to do something else*) **What would you prefer the client did instead?**

Code as follows:

paid work 1
work training scheme 2
voluntary work 3
FE college 4
stay at home 5
attend a day centre 6
combination of the above (state) 7
other 9
don't know ....X ....

S6V38 **Can you tell me something about his/her interests or hobbies - the things the client likes doing - and who he/she does them with?**

Activity	*Place*	*Who with*
....	....	....
....	....	....
....	....	....

S6V39 **Are there other things you would like him/her to do but he/she does not get the chance to do?**

Activity	*Reason for not doing it*
....	....
....	....
....	....

S6V41 **Comment on the channels of communication between yourself and the service(s) provided for .... (client)**

Code using 1-5 scale

S6V42 **Thinking about the future: What kinds of additional support do you think are needed (a) soon and (b) in the long term for .... (client)? For example:**

1. Long-term residential care in the near future?
2. Long-term care, not immediately or in the near future, but perhaps in a few year's time?
3. Just knowing that if anything should happen to me a place in a residential home would be available?
4. Additional support to enable .... (client) to remain at a home should anything happen to me?

And/or:

5. Short term respite care
6. Holiday periods
7. Weekends
8. Emergencies (any time)
9. Other (state)

Tick which apply and comment (code by circling numbers: 1 2 3 4 5 6 7 8 9)

Schedule seven (S7) - Key staff person's views

S7V21 Accommodation

What do you think about the house/flat/hostel (or whatever form of accommodation applies) where the client lives?

Code using graded opinions as follows:

Excellent 1
Good 2
Satisfactory 3
Not good 4
Deplorable 5

In particular:

S7V21	the space available	....
S7V22	comfort	....
S7V23	company (the people the client shares with)	....
S7V24	where it is - convenience	....
S7V25	staff (where applicable)	....
S7V26	other features (indicate)	....

S7V27ff Place of main daytime activity(ies)

What do you think about .... (the place) the client attends? In particular:

	the things the client does there (specify):	
S7V27	first activity	....
S7V28	second activity	....
S7V29	third activity	....
S7V31	fourth activity	....

Code graded opinions on 1-5 scale

S7V32	the other people the client meets there: (other clients)	....
S7V33	staff there	....
S7V34	transport (how the client gets there)	....
S7V35	other things about it (specify)	....
S7V36	Have you ever thought the client would like to do something else/go somewhere else other than .... (where he/she is now)?	....

Code as follows:

the client would like to do something else 1
no, the client would like to stay where he/she is 2
other answers 9
don't know ....X ....

S7V37 (*If the client would like to do something else*) **What would you prefer the client did instead?**

Code as follows:

paid work 1
work training scheme 2
voluntary work 3
FE college 4
Stay at home 5
attend a day centre 6
combination of the above (state) 7
other 9
don't know ....X ....

S7V38 **Can you tell me something about his/her interests or hobbies - the things the client likes doing - and who he/she does it with?**

Activity	*Place*	*Who with*
....	....	....
....	....	....
....	....	....

S7V39 **Are there other things you would like him/her to do but he/she does not get the chance to do?**

Activity	*Reason for not doing it*
....	....
....	....
....	....

FEATURES OF PERFORMANCE

Home/work/centre *(circle which applies)*

Completed by (social worker/researcher) ....
with ....for (client) ....

Each question deals with a specific group of tasks. A 'yes' or 'no' is firstly required for whether the task is undertaken without support or assistance. If the answer is 'no'. then a more detailed answer is required to specify more precisely what is and is not accomplished, and the degree of support or assistance required. 'Assistance' in this context means actual physical help. 'Support' means encouragement, watching, persuading or whatever, other than physical help. Some people may need very little 'assistance' but a great deal of 'support'. Others may need little 'support' but some 'assistance' for a particular part of the task (e.g. doing up a shoe lace).

In giving detailed comments, it may be useful to ask 'what's it like (say) getting dressed in the morning (or, say, after swimming) with .... In what ways does he/she need help? The tasks can also serve as cues.

Self-management skills

S3V21 **Dressing** **(21)**

Yes, can accomplish adequately and without assistance/support 1
Yes, but to accomplish adequately requires assistance/support 2
Possibly, but does not, in fact, do so 3
No 4
Other definite answers 9
Not answered X

Detailed comment only if answer above coded 2-9

Tasks:
putting clothes on
getting clothes on correctly
putting shoes on (tying lace)
holding arms ready
taking clothes off
adjusting clothes to look respectable

Assistance needed:

Staffing implications:

Support needed:

Resource/equipment implications

Comment on progress during past year

S3V22 **Wash, bath and toilet** **(22)**

Yes, can accomplish adequately and without assistance/support 1
Yes, but to accomplish adequately requires assistance/support 2
Possibly, but does not, in fact, do so 3
No 4
Other definite answers 9
Not answered 0

Tasks:

- prepare for wash
- wash hands and face
- wash hair
- brush teeth
- get in and out of bath
- wash in bath
- get dried
- use toilet
- hold soap

Assistance needed:

Staffing implications:

Support needed:

Resource/equipment implications

Comment on progress during past year

S3V23 Eating and drinking **(23)**

Yes, can accomplish adequately and
without assistance/support..............1
Yes, but to accomplish adequately
requires assistance/support 2
Possibly, but does not, in fact, do so 3
No...4
Other definite answers 9
Not answered 0

Detailed comment only if answer above coded 2-9

Tasks: eat food by himself/herself
use knife/fork/spoon
drink from cup
spoon fed with solids/all food liquidised

Assistance needed: *Staffing implications:*

Support needed: *Resource/equipment implications*

Comment on progress during past year

S3V24 Mobility **(24)**

Yes, can accomplish adequately and
without assistance/support..............1
Yes, but to accomplish adequately
requires assistance/support 2
Possibly, but does not, in fact, do so 3
No...4
Other definite answers 9
Not answered 0

Detailed comment only if answer above coded 2-9

Tasks:
- walk indoors (how far)
- walk outdoors (how far)
- up stairs
- down stairs

Assistance needed:

Staffing implications:

Support needed:

Resource/equipment implications

Comment on progress during past year

S3V25 Communication (by whatever means) **(25)**

Can he/she understand and be understood by strangers and express choices (to strangers)?

Yes, can accomplish adequately and without assistance/support 1
Yes, but to accomplish adequately requires assistance/support 2
Possibly, but does not, in fact, do so 3
No 4
Other definite answers 9
Not answered 0

Detailed comment only if answer above coded 2-9

Tasks:
- express choices relating to food
- express choices relating to clothing
- express choices in where to go
- make basic needs known (e.g. need for toilet, a drink of water)
- respond to simple requests
- can only do these things with people he/she knows really well

Assistance needed:

Staffing implications:

Support needed: *Resource/equipment implications*

Comment on progress during past year

Daily living skills

S3V26 Preparation of food/drink **(26)**

(a) Cold snack, i.e. sandwich and glass of milk

Yes, can accomplish adequately and
without assistance/support 1
Yes, but to accomplish adequately
requires assistance/support 2
Possibly, but does not, in fact, do so 3
No 4
Other definite answers 9
Not answered 0

Detailed comment only if answer above coded 2-9

Tasks: can butter sliced loaf
put sandwich together
pour out drink
add water, if necessary, to liquid

Assistance needed: *Staffing implications:*

Support needed: *Resource/equipment implications*

Comment on progress during past year

S3V27 Preparation of food/drink **(27)**

(b) Hot snack, i.e. beans on toast and hot drink

Yes, can accomplish adequately and
without assistance/support..............1
Yes, but to accomplish adequately
requires assistance/support 2
Possibly, but does not, in fact, do so 3
No..4
Other definite answers 9
Not answered 0

Detailed comment only if answer above coded 2-9

Tasks:
can open tin
can put contents into saucepan
can regulate heat
can serve with toast
can make toast without repeatedly burning it
can fill up kettle
can handle hot kettle
can make a pot of tea

Assistance needed: *Staffing implications:*

Support needed: *Resource/equipment implications*

Comment on progress during past year (or since first monitoring)

S3V28 Preparation of food/drink **(28)**

(c) A two-course cooked main meal

Yes, can accomplish adequately and
without assistance/support..............1
Yes, but to accomplish adequately
requires assistance/support 2
Possibly, but does not, in fact, do so 3

No 4
Other definite answers 9
Not answered 0

Detailed comment only if answer above coded 2-9

Tasks:
- prepare vegetables
- cook vegetables
- organise and regulate cooking for at least two items simultaneously
- make a sauce or custard
- lay table for a meal

Assistance needed:

Staffing implications:

Support needed:

Resource/equipment implications

Comment on progress during past year

S3V29 Household tasks **(29)**

Yes, can accomplish adequately and without assistance/support 1
Yes, but to accomplish adequately requires assistance/support 2
Possibly, but does not, in fact, do so 3
No 4
Other definite answers 9
Not answered 0

Detailed comment only if answer above coded 2-9

Tasks:
- make own bed
- sweep floor
- use dustpan and brush
- fill bucket with water
- use vacuum cleaner

Assistance needed:

Staffing implications:

Support needed:

Resource/equipment implications

Comment on progress during past year

S3V31 Use of money **(31)**

Yes, can accomplish adequately and
without assistance/support 1
Yes, but to accomplish adequately
requires assistance/support 2
Possibly, but does not, in fact, do so 3
No 4
Other definite answers 9
Not answered 0

Detailed comment only if answer above coded 2-9

Tasks: identify coins
select money for use
check change
management of money for weekly spending

Assistance needed:

Staffing implications:

Support needed:

Resource/equipment implications

Comment on progress during past year

S3V32 Out and about on own (by whatever means) e.g. make a journey to a place of his/her choosing, at least half a mile distant (32)

Yes, can accomplish adequately and without assistance/support..............1
Yes, but to accomplish adequately requires assistance/support 2
Possibly, but does not, in fact, do so 3
No...4
Other definite answers 9
Not answered 0

Detailed comment only if answer above coded 2-9

Tasks:
can find way if lost
can repeat a journey if he/she is familiar enough with the road/street
cannot go any further than the bus stop
understands likely dangers (e.g. traffic lights or warning signs)
does/does not have sufficient initiative to want to go out

Assistance needed:

Staffing implications:

Support needed:

Resource/equipment implications

Comment on progress during past year

S3V33 Use of public transport (i.e. generally) (33)

Yes, can accomplish adequately and without assistance/support..............1
Yes, but to accomplish adequately requires assistance/support 2
Possibly, but does not, in fact, do so 3
No...4
Other definite answers 9
Not answered 0

Detailed comment only if answer above coded 2-9

Tasks: can (only) use the one bus/train route with which he/she is familiar
can manage fares
can manage tokens or bus-pass (but not fares)
understands where to get on a bus
understands where to get off a bus

Assistance needed: *Staffing implications:*

Support needed: *Resource/equipment implications*

Comment on progress during past year

S3V34 Understanding of time

Yes, can understand without
assistance/support 1
Yes, but requires assistance/support 2
Possibly, but does not, in fact, do so 3
No 4
Other definite answers 9
Not answered 0

Detailed comment only if answer above coded 2-9

Tasks: able to tell the time using watch with hands/digital
some understanding of short time space (e.g. minutes, half an hour)
some understanding of longer time span (e.g. afternoon, day, week)

Assistance needed: *Staffing implications:*

Support needed: *Resource/equipment implications*

Comment on progress during past year

Social learning

S3V34 Ability to respond to needs/wishes of others **(34)**

Good in this respect, i.e. shows consistent awareness of the needs of others 34
Shows some awareness, but not consistently 2
Possibly, but little opportunity for this to be tested 3
Little or no awareness in this respect 4
Other answers 9
No answer given 0

Detailed comment only if answer above coded 2-9

Tasks: can do/stop doing something when asked
shows some awareness of the needs of others in daily living situations, but limited ability to respond
responds in certain situations only (explain)

Assistance needed: *Staffing implications:*

Support needed: *Resource/equipment implications*

Comment on progress during past year

Further questions on progress during past year

What progress has .... made, that you can recall, in relation to: (give examples)

a. helping at home (or managing on his/her own at home)

b. Recreational activities (including sports, swimming etc.)

c. Social activities and mixing with others

d. Basic education

e. Communicating with others and general confidence

S3V35 Is there anything specific that you can recall that .... has learnt (during the past year) that is useful to him/her in daily living? Where and how has this been learnt?

Yes, and useful in daily living 1
Yes, but not useful in daily living 2
No, probably nothing learnt 3
No, definitely nothing learnt..................4
Other answers 9
Not answered 0

Comments:

S3V36 Has there been not only a lack of progress but regression in some respects? **(36)**

Yes 1
No 2
Other answer 9

Explain:

Summary and comments:

Key to network diagrams

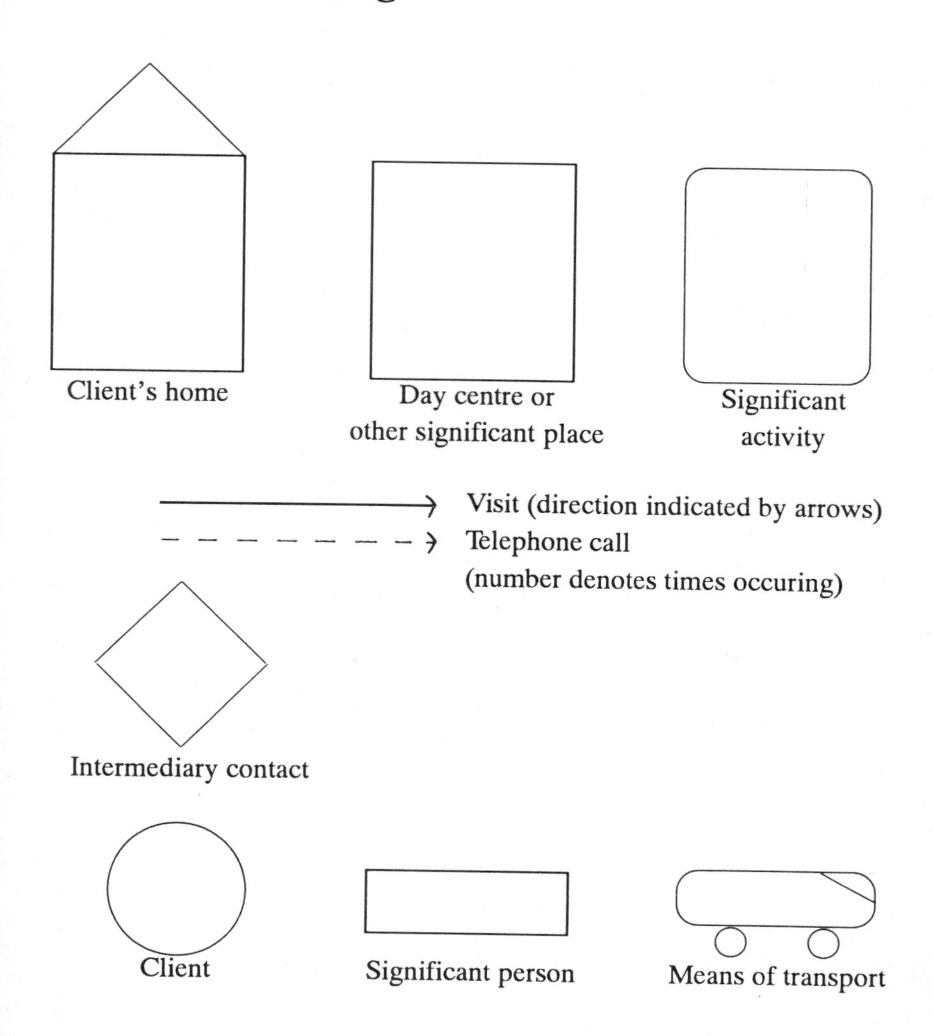

Index

Case Studies for Practice

Series Editor: Philip Seed

This series draws together case material from social research to illuminate and explore vital issues in social work practice. Each volume in the series focuses on valuable material which has been collected in the course of research, especially research into social networks. The series is intended to be particularly useful for students on CQSW and CSS courses as well as for in-service training. At the same time, it discusses issues of concern to policy makers and practitioners.

Day Services for People with Mental Handicaps 2nd edition

Compiled by Philip Seed

ISBN 1 85302 039 7 103 pages 210 x 145 paper

Case Studies for Practice 1

Taking a social network approach, the cases presented show the extent to which the limits of community care can be and are stretched to provide the services needed by the mentally handicapped and those who care for them. Cases are grouped to illustrate particular topics. The first chapter examines day care in the lives of two people with mental handicaps five years after leaving long-stay hospitals. Chapters two and three deal with much neglected topics: the situation of the elderly mentally handicapped, and that of their even older carers. The functioning of the day care setting is then explored, and the ambiguous role and potential exploitation of a particular group - the very mild mentally handicapped - within it. A new final chapter for this second edition broadens the field of study by examining day services in rural areas.

The book will be of interest to students of social work and to social workers themselves, particularly those in in-service training for residential and day care staff, and on CSS and CQSW courses, and all those concerned with the better management of day care services.

'It is good to be able to recommend this small and well presented volume at a time when there is a positive ferment of ideas and much sustained effort going into improving resources and creating effective networks. Illuminating and fundamental points emerge as one proceeds; the issues raised for discussion at the end of each section are of great value.'

- Link-Up

Day Services for People with Severe Handicaps

Compiled by Philip Seed

ISBN 1 85302 013 3
128 pages 210 x 145 paper

Case Studies for Practice 2

The second book in the series focuses on people with severe handicaps.The word 'severe' is used to include those who might be described in technical terms as having 'profound' or 'multiple' handicaps. In practical terms it is taken to mean people unable to perform most self-management or basic daily living tasks without substantial assistance. The book starts by contrasting the lifestyles of two teenagers with multiple handicaps. Both have cerebral palsy and are confined to wheelchairs, but in terms of background are quite different. The next section looks at broader issues, including the quality of communication between parents and the centre; the relevance of visits from the centre to other places; part-time attendance; the social function of centres; and whether educational activities at a centre can compensate for a lack of educational opportunity during schooling. After this the problem of respite for carers is studied. The closing chapters look at the different situations of individual clients: one who lives in a hostel but maintains parental contact; one who is physically fit but has a severe learning difficulty and one approaching 60 but with a degenerative condition leading to multiple disabilities.

Towards Independent Living: Issues for Different Client Groups

Compiled by Philip Seed

ISBN 1 85302 018 4 128 pages 210 x 145 paper

Case Studies for Practice 3

There is an important social dimension to preparation for independent living. It is not just about learning how to open a tin of beans. In essence it is about social relationships and developing a better quality of life through social relationships. Clients should be enabled to be appropriately dependent on others and to allow others to be appropriately dependent on them. This book explores the ways in which this can be brought about.

The first chapter considers the outcomes for a group of young people who had a history of residential child care, followed by experience in a hostel specifically intended to enable them to live 'more independently' in the community. The next chapters consider adults with special needs: first, epileptic adults during and after intensive training in a hostel, and second, a group of people who had attended an adult training centre on a part-time basis. Next there is a study of the benefits that adults who have been mentally ill can gain in learning to cope independently in society from attending a voluntary-run club at a day centre. Finally, 'independent living' is looked at in connection with the care of elderly people.

Towards Independent Living: Issues for Different Client Groups

Compiled by Philip Seed

ISBN 1 85302 018 4 128 pages 210 x 145 paper

Case Studies for Practice 3

There is an important social dimension to preparation for independent living. It is not just about learning how to open a tin of beans. In essence it is about social relationships and developing a better quality of life through social relationships. Clients should be enabled to be appropriately dependent on others and to allow others to be appropriately dependent on them. This book explores the ways in which this can be brought about.

The first chapter considers the outcomes for a group of young people who had a history of residential child care, followed by experience in a hostel specifically intended to enable them to live 'more independently' in the community. The next chapters consider adults with special needs: first, epileptic adults during and after intensive training in a hostel, and second, a group of people who had attended an adult training centre on a part-time basis. Next there is a study of the benefits that adults who have been mentally ill can gain in learning to cope independently in society from attending a voluntary-run club at a day centre. Finally, 'independent living' is looked at in connection with the care of elderly people.

HIV and AIDS: A Social Network Approach

Compiled by Roger Gaitley and edited by Philip Seed

ISBN 1 85302 025 7 128 pages 210 x 145 paper

Case Studies for Practice 4

This book examines the question of how professionals can best care for people whose HIV antibody positive status touches on so many of society's fears and taboos. Taking a social network approach, it draws on recent case material to explore the lives of people affected - directly or indirectly - by HIV and AIDS. The material comes from work in diverse areas: an agency making contact with 'rent' boys; direct work with drug users, some of whom are - or have partners who are - HIV positive; infants with HIV and their carers (including foster and adoptive parents) and the issues of confidentiality which arise; a group for relatives of people with HIV; and work exploring how potential social workers and other carers have to promote positive attitudes towards HIV and AIDS, as well as risk-free lifestyles.

By taking account of the people, activities and environments in his or her life, a total picture emerges of where a person finds key supports. The picture includes social, legal, health and interpersonal networks, describes where they complement, overlap and conflict, and illuminates the effects of the progression (if any) of the HIV infection in the person's life. The task of caring for the person, without further marginalising them in society, demands that these networks are understood and exploited to their full potential.

Victims of Confusion: Case Studies of Elderly Sufferers from Confusion and Dementia

Alyson Leslie

128 pages ISBN 1 85302 040 0 paper

Case Studies for Practice 5

The incidence of confusion and dementia amongst elderly people has reached almost epidemic proportions. It is estimated that one in twenty people aged sixty-five or over suffer from dementia, and in the over-85 population one fifth are affected. It is likely that a further substantial percentage of elderly people suffer less severe symptoms which still significantly affect their quality of life. Such problems can have an enormous impact not only on the sufferers but also on their carers. This book describes the experiences of a number of elderly sufferers and their carers and considers to what extent their care careers were influenced by the method, timing and source of their referral for service and by the role of the agency to which they were referred. The experience of people in residential respite care is also discussed as well as experiences in local authority and hospital day care settings.

Social Work in the Wake of Disaster

Compiled by David Tumelty and edited by Philip Seed

ISBN 1 85302 060 5 128 pages paper

Case Studies for Practice 6

Social work in the wake of major disasters is an area of work that has developed rapidly over the last few years. Social Service departments have offered help to the bereaved and survivors following the sinking of the *Herald of Free Enterprise*, the Kings Cross tube station fire, the Hungerford shootings, the Clapham rail crash, the Piper Alpha oil rig disaster, the Lockerbie air tragedy, the aftermath of Hillsborough, and the sinking of the *Marchioness*. This volume explores the types of help which social workers offer to those affected by a disaster, and those groups of people to whom such a service is offered. The material and case studies used are drawn largely from the experience of work carried out following the Piper Alpha disaster of 1988, when 167 oil-men lost their lives in the world's worst off-shore disaster.

The first chapter looks at the response that social services have offered in the immediate aftermath of a major incident. Chapters two and three look at the problems involved in identifying a disaster population, gathering information and initiating longer term work. Chapter four concentrates on aspects of work with the bereaved. Chapter five looks specifically at the needs and problems of those who survive a major disaster, and chapters six and seven develop these themes by looking at the role and functions of individual counselling and group work with the bereaved and survivors. Chapter eight looks at its function, content and distribution in the wake of a disaster. The final chapter looks at the possibilities for counselling after non-spectacular accidents.

Respite: A Social Network Approach

Philip Seed

ISBN 1 85302 061 3 paper

Case Studies for Practice 7

Of related interest

How to Get Equipment for Disability

Compiled by Michael Mandelstam

ISBN 1 85302 095 8 250 paper

This important new book is set to become an essential reference source for anyone prescribing, advising or choosing from the vast range of equipment now available. Written under the auspices of the Disabled Living Foundation and the Nuffield Provincial Hospitals Trust, *How to Get Equipment for Disability* provides detailed information on

- what type of equipment is available
- who prescribes it
- what professionals are involved
- the referral procedure
- supply and delivery
- maintenance and follow-up.

The book will prove invaluable to GPs, district nurses, occupational therapists, physiotherapists, speech therapists, community nurses, health visitors, continence advisers, social workers, rehabilitation and mobility officers, consultants, ward sisters, environmental health officers, housing improvement officers, special education needs advisers and teachers, employment service DAS teams, residential and nursing home owners, and disabled people and their carers. All sections deal with regulations, legislation, circulars, White Papers and government reports in England and Wales, Scotland and Northern Ireland. The guide also includes a comprehensive directory of manufacturers and suppliers.

CONTENTS. PART I - 1. Daily living. 2. Housing adaptations. 3. Home nursing equipment. 4. Mobility equipment (a) wheelchairs (b) walking aids (c) vehicle scheme. 5. Footwear. 6. Orthotic equipment. 7. Prosthetic appliances. 8. Incontinence appliances. 9. Dental appliances. 10. Optical appliances. 11. Oxygen/respiratory equipment. 12. Renal dialysis equipment. 13. Diabetic equipment. 14. Hearing aids. 15. Stoma appliances. 16. Communication aids. 17. Residential home provision. 18. Private nursing home provision. 19. Medical equipment (in general) provision. 20. Educational provision of equipment. 21. Employment provision. PART II - Directory of manufacturers and suppliers.

Published by Jessica Kingsley Publishers and Kogan Page for the Disabled Living Foundation